DIRK GENTLY'S
HOLISTIC DETECTIVE AGENCY

by JAMES GOSS & ARVIND ETHAN DAVID
BASED ON THE NOVEL BY DOUGLAS ADAMS

WWW.SAMUELFRENCH.CO.UK
WWW.SAMUELFRENCH.COM

Copyright © 2016 by James Goss and Arvind Ethan David
All Rights Reserved

DIRK GENTLY'S HOLISTIC DETECTIVE AGENCY is fully protected under the copyright laws of the British Commonwealth, including Canada, the United States of America, and all other countries of the Copyright Union. All rights, including professional and amateur stage productions, recitation, lecturing, public reading, motion picture, radio broadcasting, television and the rights of translation into foreign languages are strictly reserved.

ISBN 978-0-573-11122-8

www.samuelfrench.co.uk / www.samuelfrench.com

Cover art and design by Robert Hack with Stephen Downer

FOR AMATEUR PRODUCTION ENQUIRIES

UNITED KINGDOM AND WORLD EXCLUDING NORTH AMERICA
plays@SamuelFrench-London.co.uk
020 7255 4302/01

UNITED STATES AND CANADA
info@SamuelFrench.com
1-866-598-8449

Each title is subject to availability from Samuel French, depending upon country of performance.

CAUTION: Professional and amateur producers are hereby warned that DIRK GENTLY'S HOLISTIC DETECTIVE AGENCY is subject to a licensing fee. Publication of this play does not imply availability for performance. Both amateurs and professionals considering a production are strongly advised to apply to the appropriate agent before starting rehearsals, advertising, or booking a theatre. A licensing fee must be paid whether the title is presented for charity or gain and whether or not admission is charged.

The professional rights in this play are controlled by United Agents LLP, 12-26 Lexington Street, London, W1F OLE.

No one shall make any changes in this title for the purpose of production. No part of this book may be reproduced, stored in a retrieval system, or transmitted in any form, by any means, now known or yet to be invented, including mechanical, electronic, photocopying, recording, videotaping, or otherwise, without the prior written permission of the publisher. No one shall upload this title, or part of this title, to any social media websites.

The right of James Goss and Arvind Ethan David to be identified as authors of this work has been asserted in accordance with Section 77 of the Copyright, Designs and Patents Act 1988.

For PASF in memoriam, and to SGAH, AGM, SHCR and all the teachers at Stowe School, who believed in two improbable teenagers.

A proportion of all revenue from the book sales and performance fees from this play will be donated to Save the Rhino International, of which Douglas Adams was a founding patron. Save the Rhino International's vision is for all five rhino species to thrive in the wild for future generations.

INTRODUCTION

Welcome to the play of *Dirk Gently's Holistic Detective Agency*. The light works, the gravity works. Everything else we take our chances with.

After *The Hitchhiker's Guide to the Galaxy*, Douglas Adams went on to create Dirk Gently, a detective with a belief in the fundamental interconnectedness of all things, a unique relationship with the laws of probability, and a love of cats and pizza. In *Dirk Gently's Holistic Detective Agency* (the first of two Dirk books, Douglas was working on a third, *The Salmon of Doubt*, when he died in 2001) Dirk finds himself on the trail of a gruesome murderer who is fundamentally interconnected with the works of Coleridge, quantum physics and the enigmatic study of the Cambridge Professor of Chronology. It is on this adventure that the play is based.

*

For us, it started at boarding school, and we were asked to direct the school play. Unable to find anything we wanted to put on (mainly because we were too lazy to actually *read* anything) we decided, with the careless hubris of teenagers, to adapt a novel. Not just any novel of course, but *Dirk Gently's Holistic Detective Agency*, a novel with a ludicrously complicated plot which spans four billion years, at least three alternative universes; a cast comprising vampire-detectives, aliens and ghosts and an electric monk; all linked by the central theme of "the fundamental interconnectedness of all things" (hence 'holistic').

We were sixteen, so didn't bother to get rights clearance but just staged the thing. It was very short (about an hour) and by all accounts, amusing but utterly incomprehensible. It had a budget of forty pounds. A video recording of this production exists, but no one is sure exactly why.

Somehow, though, within the narrow confines of school cloisters, the play was a huge, popular success. As such, it was a changing point in our school careers: too clever by half, overly academic, poetry quoting, playwriting adolescents seldom win popularity contests in British boarding schools; somehow, however *Dirk's* popular appeal spread to us, and suddenly, unexpectedly, we had street-cred.

Fast-forward three years: we're undergrads at Oxford, trying to make our mark on the University drama scene. *Dirk* once again comes to mind, and a re-written, re-vamped production, rife with special effects, is born. This time, we figure we should get permission from Douglas's agents – and being the terribly gracious Ed Victor and Maggie Phillips, they give it. More surprisingly, they come to see the show, and, enjoy it so much they tell Douglas that he must see it, too – and on the penultimate night, the great man does. Even more unexpectedly: he loves it.

Later that night, over Moroccan lamb, red wine and the adrenalin from meeting one of our idols, Douglas opened and then blew away our minds with conversation about theatre and the Internet, writing comedy and science fiction, and the joy of collaborative creation. In retrospect, that night marked the beginning of our careers. It was when we started making up stories for a living.

In the years since, much to our surprise, there has come a seemingly never-ending series of requests, from across the globe, to perform the play. Somehow the global

Douglas Adams mafia had heard of the script's existence, they ferreted pirate sections across the wilderness of the Internet, and then started to email us. From Minnesota and Melbourne, from Buenos Aeries and Didcot, from universities and schools, from amateur dramatic groups and Douglas fan clubs, requests kept coming. As such, the play constantly got re-written and (hopefully) improved.

More than twenty years later, and the play is being published to join the many manifestations of *Dirk Gently* now in the world: comics, multiple television shows as well as novelisations and podcasts of Douglas's lost *Doctor Who* episodes that inspired Dirk in the first place. That the two of us, whose careers started that night with Douglas, have been involved as writers, editors and/or producers of most of the versions since, is as wonderful as it was unforeseeable.

Arthur Conan Doyle wrote, about another detective, that "talent immediately recognizes genius"; our little adolescent talents recognized the genius of Dirk Gently, and we've been lucky to ride shotgun with him throughout our lives.

It is a remarkable thing for one author, and one fictional character to have such a lasting and direct effect on so many for so long – for whilst our story might be one of the most extreme cases of Douglas Adams's influence, fourteen years after his death, it is increasingly clear how much today's generation of science fiction and comedy writers and filmmakers owes him.

Such positive influence is something we would have liked to have thanked Douglas for in life. Denied that chance, perhaps this public acknowledgement makes small recompense.

Douglas's response, though, might be predicted: a modest shrug of his giant shoulders and the riposte that it wasn't him we should thank, but just the "fundamental interconnectedness of all things…"

Arvind Ethan David & James Goss

Arvind Ethan David is a producer and writer of film, television, theatre and comic books. In addition to the multiple manifestations of *Dirk Gently*, he is best known for his collaborations with David Baddiel on the film and musical versions of *The Infidel*. He lives in Los Angeles with his wife, and their (entirely alive, if utterly insane) cat, Olive.

James Goss has written novels, plays and audio dramas, but only *Dirk* haunts him. It's younger, funnier, and it's always going to more interesting places than him. In an effort to settle the score, he's novelised two Douglas Adams television scripts – *City of Death* and *The Pirate Planet*. He's making sure that, like him, they stay firmly on the shelf.

PRODUCTION NOTES

When you have a play with a time span of four billion years, a cast that includes ghosts, aliens and Cambridge dons, and a study that travels through space/time at the drop of an abacus, you have to be a little inventive.

Here are a few suggestions for its staging. Feel free to interpret them according to your means and whims.

Screen

Some of the more out-there scenes greatly benefit from having the resources of a screen and a projector. What you project on the screen depends rather on your budget and available skills. Here are three points on the spectrum:

1. Produce a series of short animated sequences, incorporating your live action cast – you'll find your animators get very excited by the "beginning of life" and "time travel" sequences.

2. Using slides, photographs, drawings, e.g. of an alien space craft, a huge explosion, a close up of a salt cellar in a pot, a horse in a bathroom.

3. If no screen, then lighting, loud noise and smoke.

This text throughout assumes the full, FAT experience.

Set design

Set design also provides something of a challenge when your locations range from prehistoric earth, the inside of a bubble of stasis and a horse-filled bathroom. Sorry about that. Again, the screen is helpful, but however designed, the set should include spaces which can serve as:

1. **Reg's study** – a cosy sofa, lamp, and chair scenario, with a coffee table, prominent on which is an abacus. A hatch leads to a kitchen, a staircase leads to a bathroom.

2. **Dirk's office** – two desks (Dirk's and his secretary Janice's), chairs, a light, hat-stand, and telephones.

3. **Susan's flat** – a cello (or other suitable musical instrument) and a sofa plus an old-fashioned answerphone.

4. **Richard's flat** – living room and computer-filled study, linked by a staircase which is partially blocked by a (firmly wedged) sofa.

5. A large central area which passes for halls/roads/cars/breathing space.

Conjuring tricks

This is a play in which close-up magic plays an important part. In an ideal world, all the conjuring tricks from Reg and Dirk should be properly and expertly performed using skill, charm and extreme legerdemain. Unless you are lucky enough to have Neil Patrick Harris in your cast, some boning up on basic sleight-of-hand techniques may be necessary.

Use of music

The relationship between music (in particular the music of Johann Sebastian Bach), mathematics and the natural world is central to the plot of the novel. Dramatic imperatives, sadly, have made this rather less so in the play. Nevertheless, the choice of music is important, and we have indicated appropriate pieces at various points in the text.

Further, it is important that the actress playing Susan Way is an accomplished classical musician. In both novel and play script, she is a cellist. If casting limitations rule this out, a violinist, a harpist, a pianist or even a flautist will all do as well, as long as music choices are made intelligently. Hell, if she's *really* good, she can play the bongos. References to musical instruments in the dialogue and stage directions should be adapted accordingly.

DRAMATIS PERSONAE

DIRK GENTLY – *a holistic detective*
JANICE PEARCE – *Dirk's secretary*
"**REG**", Professor Urban Chronotis – *Regius Professor of Chronology, University of Cambridge*
RICHARD MacDUFF – *a coder*
GORDON WAY – *a (late) tech magnate*
SUSAN WAY – *a musician, Gordon's sister*
MICHAEL WENTON-WEAKES – *A (fired) magazine editor. Possessed.*
SERGEANT GILKS – *A plainclothes police detective*
*****PERKINS** – *A policeman*
*****ALBERT ROSS** – *Editor, Fathom Magazine*
SARAH ANDROYD – *a little girl*
*****MARVIN ANDROYD** – *her father*
*****WATKIN** – *a don*
*****GORDON'S HOUSEKEEPER**
*****WAITRESS, *BRIDE, *GROOM, *WEDDING GUESTS, *DONS, *GHOSTS, *ALIENS**, etc
HORSE

* *Denotes parts which are easily doubled up*

ACT ONE
Scene One, Scene Two, Scene Three, Scene Four,
Scene Five, Scene Six

ACT TWO
Scene One, Scene Two, Scene Three, Scene Four,
Scene Five, Scene Six

ACT THREE
Scene One, Scene Two, Scene Three, Scene Four,
Scene Five, Scene Six, Scene Seven, Scene Eight, Scene Nine

EPILOGUE
Scene Ten

ACT ONE

Scene One

On screen: Animation Title Sequence – Like Star Wars, but done with blu-tac and felt tip pens.

"Douglas Adams's

DIRK GENTLY'S

HOLISTIC

DETECTIVE

AGENCY..."

DIRK *stands in darkness.*

He is dressed entirely in a long dark blue leather jacket, a red hat which fails to harmonise with it, and a suit which fails to harmonise with either: somehow he makes it cool. He is lit as he strikes a match. He speaks with an accent so British it could be Eastern European.

DIRK That with music loud and long,
I would build that dome in air,
That sunny dome! Those caves of ice!
And all who heard should see them there,
And all should cry, Beware! Beware!
His flashing eyes, his floating hair!
Weave a circle round him thrice,
And close your eyes with holy dread,
For he on honey dew hath fed,
And drunk the milk of paradise.

DIRK *begins to move, talking as he goes, a spotlight follows him.*

It's beautiful is it not? It's Coleridge. Samuel Taylor. Poet. Ever wonder what – or who – was going through his mind when he wrote it? And what, if you will forgive, does it mean? Not the most exciting of mysteries, you might think, yet things are seldom what they seem. And little questions sometimes have big answers.

DIRK, *at the bottom of the stairs, makes a grand gesture with his arms. As he speaks, lights up on* **DIRK**'s *office, stage right. Office sounds inter-mingling with more out-of-this world ones: howling wind, whirring photocopier, the screech of a hawk, the clattering of a typewriter, the neighing of a horse, the ringing of a telephone…*

Welcome, Ladies and Gentlemen. These are the offices of Dirk Gently's Holistic Detective Agency – Dirk Gently, owner and proprietor, at your service *(pause)*. Thank you for asking; the term "holistic" refers to my belief in the fundamental interconnectedness of all things.

I do not concern myself with such petty things as fingerprint powder, tell-tale pieces of pocket fluff or inane footprints. I see the solution to each problem as being detectable in the pattern and web of the whole.

It is an oft-repeated cliché, ladies and gentleman, that the flapping of a butterfly's wings in the Sahara may precipitate a tsunami in South Wales – but precious few have realised how many lives would be saved if that butterfly's frivolous flapping could be stopped. Such is my burden: such is my destiny.

Some of the events which you are about to see may strike you as fantastical and tangential – chalk that up to your rough-and-ready understanding of the physical world. Everything matters.

Dance with me to the waltz of causation. In time you will understand many things. Even my expenses. Which are necessary and non-negotiable.

On screen:

CAPTION: FOUR BILLION YEARS AGO… FRIDAY.

A desolate, alien landscape gradually appears – the camera pans across rocks and boulders. The sky is bleak and forbidding. Nothing is living here.

This time there will be no witnesses, except for you and me. This time there will just be the dead earth, a rumble of thunder, and the onset of that interminable drizzle from the north-east by which so many of the world's most momentous events seem to be accompanied.

With an even grander gesture, **DIRK** *sweeps off, stage right.*

On screen: The sky crackles with clouds, and there is rain. As the haze clears we begin to hear garbled radio instructions in an alien tongue. We see a spaceship, perched on a cliff edge.

The stage is suddenly flooded by bizarrely dressed characters, clad in a strange cross between space-suits and scuba diving kit. They are shouting from 'Kubla Khan' with some urgency.

The stage is flooded by smoke. A low, keening, electronic whine builds.

On screen: The spaceship lifts itself off the ground, and hovers in a gathering electrical storm. There is a growing sound of tortured engines, building ominously. The ship hovers over the ground, distorts, and the whining noise oscillates. There is a blaring explosion which whites out the screen.

On stage: The chants cut off abruptly and there is darkness and silence.

Scene Two

A bell tolls.

On screen caption: Senior Common Room, Thursday evening, Four billion years later. St. Cedd's College, Cambridge.

A number of formally clad guests at a pre-dinner drinks. They include: **MARVIN ANDROYD**, *a BBC Radio producer,* **SARAH ANDROYD**, *his eight-year-old daughter, numerous Professors (***DONS**, *in Cambridge speak), including* **WATKIN**, *and a* **WAITRESS** *who moves amongst them, dispensing drinks.*

DIRK *enters, unnoticed by the party. Most of his lines in this scene are directed to the audience. During these monologues the rest of the stage action freezes, coming back to life when he finishes. Except where specifically indicated by the text,* **DIRK** *is invisible to the other characters during this scene.*

DIRK St. Cedd's College, Cambridge. Founded in the year something or other, by someone I forget in honour of someone whose name for the moment escapes me.

WAITRESS St. Cedd, sir?

DIRK *takes a drink from the tray.*

DIRK Do you know, I probably think it was. One of the duller Northumbrian saints, His brother Chad was even duller – has a cathedral in Birmingham if that gives you some idea. My old college, as it happens, though my memories of my days there are not entirely uncomplicated.

Enter **RICHARD** *stage left. He is wearing a coat and dinner suit. He is cold. He is waiting for someone.* **PROFESSOR REG CHRONOTIS**, *enters stage right similarly but far more shabbily dressed. They see each other. Pause. And recognise each other.*

REG Ah, Young MacDuff! How splendid.

On screen: Close-up surveillance photographs of Professor Urban Chronotis, from a variety of angles.

DIRK Professor Urban Chronotis, Regius Professor of Chronology. I only met him once during my time at St. Cedd's...

RICHARD Professor! *(they shake hands)*

REG Dear fellow. I am so glad you could come. Grateful of company for special college dinners. One always hopes it will aid the digestion. Never does, of course.

RICHARD Umm.

REG Come, come, Richard. May I call you Richard? I've always believed it is the privilege of tutors to patronise their graduates.

They join the main party. All freeze.

On screen: Surveillance shots of **RICHARD**.

DIRK Richard MacDuff was my roommate eight years ago. He was a credulous fellow, who, if the truth were known, I selected specially for his credulity. A credulous roomate is invaluable if one wishes to become infamous. You see, Richard was kind, well, gullible enough to believe every rumour that I had occasion to deny about myself. More importantly, he never attempted to find out what the source of these rumours was – if not my own outraged denials.

It started innocently enough. A cult of personality is a useful thing to have within the confines of a small college. It was easy enough to strenuously deny that my family came from the smarter end of Transylvania. Painfully simple to make clear that I had not inherited any psychic powers whatsoever from my mother's side. It was absolute nonsense that there were any bats of any kind within the family tree, and the reason for my hanging upside down from the rafters at all hours was an inherited back complaint.

On screen: College yearbook shots of **DIRK**. *He appears ghoulish, drinking blood from a skull, in dark prayer over a black candle, and dangling upside-down. Beaming.*

REG ...of course, whenever I'm called on to tutor – one hesitates to say teach – I take the wise precaution of removing all the books on my reading list from the libraries...

The party all freeze.

DIRK By means of a whole chain of such strategically deployed denials of the most exotic and exciting rumours, I was able to create, and deny, the myth that I was a mystic, telepathic, clairvoyant, psychosassic vampire bat.

WAITRESS *(proffering drinks)* Red or white, sir?

DIRK Red, of course. *(Takes wine. Drinks with toothy relish)* Psychosassic was my own word, and I strenuously denied that it meant anything at all. Nevertheless, there was a time when it was advantageous for people to think that it did. But that was eight years ago.

REG *(to* **RICHARD***)* Coleridge, Samuel Taylor. Poet. I expect you've heard of him. Favoured son of the college, despite his fondness for recreational pharmaceuticals. This is his dinner. Well, not literally of course, it would be cold by now. Here have some salt. *(He takes salt from side table)*

All freeze.

DIRK One night eight years ago, MacDuff heard me talking in my sleep. *(Takes a pillow from a passing tray, and mumbles into it)* 'The opening up of trade routes to the mumble mumble burble was the turning point for the growth of empire in the snore footle mumble... Discussszzzzz' Well, finalists will snatch at any hope, even believing that someone can clair-audiently predict exam papers, simply because they claim – sorry, deny – to come from the smarter end of Transylvania, are denied to be psychosassic, and refute sleep talking about Schleswig-Holstein and Derrida.

What was the harm in that? It cheered me up to be wined and dined at great expense in the hope that in my drunken slumbers I would become verbose about, say *(into pillow)* "The tectonic... murmur... of the... gurgle... bottle fly... snore.". News, however, spread quietly, discreetly, and like wildfire. Until, to conclusively deny everything, I was forced to write, under hypnosis, a set of Finals papers, only because it would once and for all scotch the whole silly – immensely, tediously silly – business. The papers would be locked away, and only examined after Finals. The entire project was of purely academic interest. No money would change hands. No money whatsoever. But that was before my mother developed a need to undergo extensive dental surgery. In Transylvania.

The party unfreezes.

REG *(offering a heavy silver salt cellar)* Go on, have some salt.

RICHARD Er – thank you, I think I'll wait.

REG Go on, take it.

REG *performs an over-flamboyant and none-too-subtle piece of close-up magic: as* **RICHARD** *goes to take the salt cellar, it vanishes.*

Good one, eh? Magic tricks are still my special hobby. Irritating, I know, but next on my list for giving up after smoking and leeches.

The party freezes.

DIRK Whereas my special hobby was pseudo-clairvoyance. My special talent, like the Professor's own, proved to be far, far rarer...

SARAH *(the little girl) has been bored for a considerable amount of time. She unfreezes and runs up to* **DIRK**. *She kicks him smartly on the shin. The party unfreezes.*

REG So, Richard, a glowing career in personal computers... for the famous Gordon Way, yes? If I can remember, and I very much doubt I can, did you not have a computer when you were here?

RICHARD Yes, as a matter of fact I did. That's actually why I never handed in an essay.

REG Really? Nowadays computers have made undergraduates sickeningly efficient. They even hand their essays in "on the cloud", so one can no longer claim to have lost them. Most regrettable. So, how were you refreshingly able to use your computer to avoid writing essays?

RICHARD I was teaching it how to play "Three Blind Mice".

REG For three years? Splendid, I really must suggest it to a few of my students.

RICHARD Well, it'd be child's play now. What we called a computer then was really a kind of electric abacus, but...

REG Oh, now don't underestimate the abacus. In skilled hands it's a very sophisticated calculating device. Furthermore, it requires no power, can be made of any materials, and never goes "bing" in the middle of an important piece of work.

RICHARD *looks round the room and notices* **SARAH**, *the little girl.*

RICHARD By the way, who's that?

REG Who's what?

RICHARD The girl. The very, very little girl. Is it some new maths professor?

REG Do you know – I haven't the faintest idea. Never known anything like it. How extraordinary.

SARAH *has been misbehaving for some time now, and is currently crawling about on the floor pulling on the trailing gowns of the* **DONS**.

MARVIN Stop that!

SARAH *stops, pauses and then starts again, blowing a raspberry at her father's back.*

REG Poor child, there isn't a don in this room who doesn't behave exactly like that inside. Pity you didn't bring your computer with you. It might have cheered up the poor young lady. A quick burst of "Three Blind Mice" might have done much to relieve her spirits. *(to* **SARAH***)* Hello.

SARAH Hello!

REG Which do you think is worse? The wine or the company?

SARAH *laughs.*

I think you're wise not to commit yourself at this stage. Myself, I'm waiting for the actual meal before I make any judgements. They've been boiling the carrots since the weekend, but I fear it may not be enough. The only thing that could possibly be worse than the carrots is Watkin. He's the man with the big nose standing over there amongst those other men with big noses. My name's Reg, by the way, come over and kick me when you have a moment.

SARAH You're funny.

SARAH *kicks* **REG** *and runs away.* **DONS** *turn round and stare at her. All freeze.*

DIRK The exam papers I produced under hypnosis, I had pieced together simply by doing the same minimum research that any student doing exams should do; studying previous exam papers and making intelligent guesses. I was pretty sure of getting a strike rate that was sufficiently high to satisfy the credulous and sufficiently low for the whole exercise to look perfectly innocent. As indeed, it was.

The party unfreezes.

RICHARD ...Working for Gordon Way's quite interesting. Gordon's better and worse than the press make him out to be. I like him a lot, actually. Like any driven man he can be a bit trying at times, but I've known him since the start. He's fine. But driven men are very enthusiastic. It's just that it's not a good idea to let him have your phone number.

REG What? Why's that?

RICHARD When he has ideas he has to talk them out to whoever will listen. Or, if the people themselves are not available, which is increasingly the case, their voicemail will do just as well. He's the only person who still uses my landline. He just rings it up and talks to it. He's had an old-fashioned answering machine installed at all his closest friends' homes. He has one secretary whose sole job is to collect tapes from people he might have phoned, transcribe them and give him the edited text the next day in a blue folder.

REG A blue one, eh?

RICHARD Ask me why he doesn't simply use a recorder?

REG I expect it's because he doesn't like talking to himself. There is logic there, of a kind. So tell me, where does young MacDuff fit into all this?

RICHARD Well, I head up multi-platform strategy.

REG Hmmmn. Sounds like you get paid a lot of money for "Three Blind Mice".

RICHARD Well, it's looking after all sorts of things that catch Gordon's eye. For instance he's just made me a Contributing Editor of his new magazine.

REG Yes, didn't he buy *Fathom*? A proper printed magazine. Obviously he has decided to patronise the arts, and I do mean patronise. An interesting choice for a tech magnate.

All freeze.

DIRK What led to my taking my last, rather hurried gaze, at St. Cedd's, from the window of a police car was that all the papers I sold turned out to be the same as the papers that were actually sat. Exactly the same. Word for word. To the very comma. It was at this point that I began to suspect that all things could be connected. And that even a simple trick could have the most serious consequences...

DIRK *exits. The party unfreezes.*

SARAH Please Daddy, can I now?

MARVIN Later.

SARAH This is already later, I've been timing it.

MARVIN Well...

SARAH We've been to Greece. It was beautiful. I think that Greece is the most beautiful place in the whole world. I found a pot!

Takes a dirty, small, Greek pot from her bag to a politely unenthusiastic reaction from the crowd.

MARVIN Probably nothing, you know the way it is. Everyone who goes to Greece for the first time thinks they've found a pot, don't they? Ha. Ha.

Nods of assent. The pot is passed half-heartedly around.

SARAH *(to* **WATKIN***)* You look clever – you should know.

WATKIN My dear girl, it looks about 200 years old, at the most. I would think. Very rough. Very crude example of its type, utterly without value of course.

SARAH *is crushed by this.*

REG *(to* RICHARD*)* Sour lot. *(To* SARAH*)* Young lady, would you care to regard this simple salt cellar? *(Produces salt cellar, and beckons* SARAH *over)*

WATKIN Not again you old fool!

REG Regard this simple hat.

SARAH You haven't got a hat. *(On the edge of tears)*

REG Oh, a moment please.

REG *exits to get a hat.* DIRK *watches him go.*

DON 1 The only thing I ever discovered in Greece was the sublime fiction of Greek ferry timetables. Wonderful fantasy.

Chorus of agreement.

DON 2 Better than Yeats.

REG *re-enters with a hat.*

REG Regard this simple salt cellar, regard this woolly hat. I put the salt cellar in the hat, thus, and it is gone!!

Salt cellar vanishes.

SARAH That wasn't very good.

REG Ah, but wait... Young lady, you are clearly an enchantress of prodigious powers. *(He grasps pot)* I bow to you! May I show these people what you have wrought?

SARAH *nods. Uncertainly.*

With a flourish, REG *smashes the pot, revealing the salt cellar embedded in it.*

SARAH *is amazed. Even the* DONS *are a little impressed. A hush falls.*

DIRK *watches, intrigued.*

WATKIN *(steps forward, importantly)* Ladies and gentlemen, tonight is a special night in the annals of our college. The Coleridge dinner. In honour of the occasion, I ask you all to join me in a toast to Coleridge. To Coleridge! *(Raises glass)*

If you would like to come through and take your places for dinner.

As is traditional on this occasion, Coleridge's unfinished masterpiece, Kubla Khan, will now be read.

All troop off stage as **DIRK** *takes it upon himself to perform the reading.*

DIRK In Xanadu did Kubla Khan...

A stately pleasure dome decree,

Where Alpha, the sacred River ran,

In caverns measureless to man,

Down to a sunless sea.

Scene Three

SUSAN*'s flat. In the corner is an old fashioned landline and vintage answerphone.*

SUSAN *is dressed formally for dinner. Clearly in a state of some agitation, she strums haphazardly on her cello, plays with her mobile and generally frets.*

DIRK *reclines, Cheshire cat-like, on the coffee table. He is invisible to* SUSAN. *There is a pot of tea. He pours himself a cup and sips.*

DIRK   A damsel with a dulcimer

    In a vision once I saw:

    It was an Abyssinian maid,

    And on her dulcimer she played,

    Singing of Mount Abora.

    Who is this vision of woman? This dulcimer wielding damsel? Talented, beautiful...

SUSAN   Damn you, Richard!

DIRK   Very, very, annoyed.

SUSAN   Even allowing for traffic, mishaps, and general vagueness and dilatoriness, it's now well over half an hour past the time you insisted was the latest time we could possibly afford to leave. I got ready early. No idea why. *(She stares at her phone)* And no, I'm not going to text to ask where the hell you are. It's admitting defeat.

SUSAN *puts the phone down and plays with her cello a little more.*

DIRK   There are two men in Susan Way's life. Her brother Gordon. And Richard MacDuff. Her brother calls her all the time. Richard... not so much.

SUSAN *stops playing the cello and stares at the phone.*

SUSAN What if something terrible has happened to you? That would explain it... no, I don't believe that for a moment. Nothing terrible ever happens to you, though I am beginning to think that it was time that something damn well did. In fact, if nothing terrible happens to Richard MacDuff soon, then maybe I'd better happen. In a terrible way. Not that I'm terrible per se. Well, he better just watch it.

SUSAN *puts the mobile phone down and plays with her cello a little more.*

Ring, damn you!

Her mobile phone does not ring. She plucks at the cello.

No. I'm not going to text.

She plucks at the cello.

Perhaps I should phone. I'll be damned if I'm going to phone. Perhaps if I phone, he'll phone me at the same time, and neither of us will be able to get through... I pretty much refuse to admit I even thought that.

Right, that's it.

She grabs the phone. Puts it down. And then picks it up again – annoyed but indecisive.

No, Richard. This is it. Really and absolutely it. Now I am going to make a call. Just not to you.

She picks up the phone, and finds a different number.

Hello, Michael? Yes, it's Susan. You said I should call you if I was free this evening, and I said I'd rather be dead in a ditch, remember? Well, I've suddenly discovered that I am free, absolutely, completely and utterly free, and there isn't a decent ditch for miles around. Make your move while you've got your chance is my advice to you. I'll be at Soho House in half an hour. By-ee.

She hangs up.

SUSAN *huffily pulls on shoes, sprays perfume over herself,* **DIRK** *enjoys the smell. She leaves,* **DIRK** *snaps his fingers and gestures towards the answerphone.*

SUSAN *returns, flicks answerphone on and leaves. As an afterthought she throws her mobile down next to the landline.*

Scene Four

REG's *study. A coffee table on which is an old wooden abacus and, carefully set out, a decanter of port and three glasses. Piles of books everywhere. A hatch opens into an off-stage kitchen and upstairs, a bathroom.*

REG *and* **RICHARD** *enter.*

REG Try and make yourself comfortable on the sofa. I don't know if you'll manage it. It always feels to me as if it's been stuffed with cabbage leaves and cutlery. Do you have a good sofa?

RICHARD *(cheered by the silliness of the question)* Well, yes.

REG Oh. Well, I wish you'd tell me where you found it. I have endless trouble with them, quite endless.

RICHARD I've never actually sat on mine.

REG Very wise, very, very wise.

RICHARD Not that I wouldn't want to. It's just the delivery men got it part way up the stairs to my new flat, got it stuck, and couldn't get it back down again. No-one can.

REG Odd. I've certainly never come across any irreversible mathematics involving sofas. Could be a new field. Have you spoken to any spatial geometricians?

RICHARD I did better than that, I've modelled the problem in three dimensions on my computer – and so far it just says no way.

On screen: An animated sofa appears. It is stuck in a stairwell, spinning in wireframe.

REG Dear me. How puzzling. But you must let me know if there is anything I can get you. Port perhaps, or brandy? The port is I think the better bet, laid down by the college in 1934, and one of the finest vintages I think you'll find, and on the other hand I don't actually have any brandy.

RICHARD Tea is what I would really like. I have to drive back up to London.

REG Indeed. Then I shall be a moment or two in the kitchen. Continue to tell me of your sofa, and do feel free in the meantime to sit on mine. Has it been stuck there long?

REG *exits to the kitchen.*

RICHARD Oh, only about three weeks. I could just saw it up and throw it away, but I can't believe that there isn't a logical answer.

Noises of kettle boiling.

The computer just refuses to offer any way of getting it out, and, worse, says it couldn't have got there in the first place. Not without fundamental restructuring of the walls. So, either there's something wrong with the fundamental structure of the matter in my walls, or there's something wrong with the program. Which would you guess?

REG *enters, smiling benevolently.*

REG I suspect, the real problem is that you have too many paper clips up your nose. *(Leaning across he pulls a chain of eleven paper clips and a small rubber swan out of* **RICHARD***'s nose. He examines the swan intently)* Ah, the real culprit. They come in cereal packets, you know, and cause no end of trouble.

REG *exits.*

RICHARD To tell you the truth, it's been a while since a program I've written has really worked. The last one was sensational. But we never sold a single download.

REG *(head through kitchen hatch)* Oh, what did it do?

RICHARD Well, it was a kind of back-to-front program. Many of the best ideas are just an old idea back-to-front. You see there have already been several programs written that help you to arrive at decisions by properly ordering and analysing all the relevant facts so that they then point naturally towards the right decision. The drawback with these is that the decision which all the properly ordered and analysed facts point to, is not necessarily the one you want.

REG *(head through kitchen hatch)* Yeeessss...

RICHARD Well, Gordon's great insight was to design a program which you told in advance, what conclusion you wanted it to reach, and then left to carefully order and analyse the facts appropriately. It worked brilliantly. Gordon was able to buy himself a Porsche almost immediately despite being completely broke and a hopeless driver. Even his bank manager was unable to find fault with his reasoning. Even when Gordon wrote the car off three weeks later.

REG So why didn't it sell?

RICHARD The entire project was bought up, lock, stock and barrel by the Pentagon... The deal put Way Forward on a very sound financial foundation. Its moral foundation, on the other hand, is not something I would want to build a beach-house on.

I've recently been analysing their strategies, and the pattern of the algorithms is quite clear. So much so, in fact, that looking at decisions over the past few years, I'm fairly sure that the US Navy is using version 2.0 while the Air Force for some reason only has the beta-test version of 1.5. Odd that.

The kettle boils.

REG Fascinating. Do excuse me. *(Exits)*

RICHARD *picks up a book on the coffee table.*

On screen: close-up of book cover, reads – "Classical Greek Pots".

RICHARD *(a piece of paper falls out. Reads, under breath)* "Regard this simple salt cellar, regard this simple hat." How very odd.

On screen: Close-up of note, scribbly handwriting on crumpled paper "Regard this simple salt cellar, regard this simple hat".

REG *(from the kitchen)* Earl Grey or Lapsang Souchong? Or Darjeeling? Or PG Tips?

RICHARD Darjeeling will do fine.

REG Milk?

RICHARD Yes, please.

REG One lump or two?

RICHARD One please.

REG Sugar?

RICHARD Er, what?

REG *(sticks head through hatch)* Just a tiny joke of mine, to check that people are really listening. *(Head exits)*

> **REG**'s *entire body re-enters carrying tea tray in elaborate ceremony, tea cosy once again on head.* **RICHARD** *hurriedly puts the note into the book and clears space on the table for the tea things.*

RICHARD Professor, there's something I've always wanted to know, but never plucked up the courage to ask you when I was an undergraduate.

REG Courage? My dear boy, it never occurred to me that I was a particularly fearsome figure. *(He puts a sugar cube in his ear and twiddles with it)* Ask away, by all means.

RICHARD Well, you are the Regius Professor of Chronology?

REG Absolutely.

RICHARD Well, what exactly *is* the Regius Professorship of Chronology?

REG Sinecure, my dear fellow, an absolute sinecure. A small amount of money for a very small, or shall we say non-existent, amount of work. That puts me permanently just ahead of the game, which is a comfortable, if frugal, place to spend your life, I recommend it. Rich tea finger?

RICHARD Thanks; but what sort of study is it supposed to be? Is it history? Physics? Philosophy? What?

REG Well, since you're interested, the chair was originally instituted by George III; who, as you know, entertained a number of amusing notions, including the belief that one of the trees in Windsor Great Park was in fact Frederick the Great.

It was his own appointment, hence Regius. George III was, as you may know, obsessed with time. Filled the palace with clocks. Wound them incessantly. Would get up in the middle of the night and prowl about in his nightshirt winding clocks.

He was very concerned that time continued to go forward, you see. So many terrible things had occurred in his life that he was terrified that any of them may happen again if time were ever allowed to slip backwards, even for a moment. A very understandable fear, especially if you're barking mad, which I'm very much afraid to say he was.

He appointed me, or rather, I should say my office, this professorship, you understand, this, er, Chair of Chronology to see if there was any particular reason why one thing happened after another, and if there was, was there any way of stopping it?

Since the answers to the three questions were, I knew immediately, yes, no and maybe, I realised that I could the take the rest of my career off.

RICHARD And your predecessors?

REG Er, they were much of the same mind.

RICHARD But who were they?

REG Who were they? Well, splendid fellows, all of them. Remind me to tell you about them, some day. See this lampshade? Wordsworth was sick over this lampshade once. Great man.

RICHARD Oh.

REG Actually, one reason I hoped you would come is so I could ask you... whatever became of that friend of yours, when you were here... do you ever see him? Odd Eastern European chap, Gently... Do you remember the fellow?

RICHARD Oh, you mean Dirk, Dirk Gently. Nope, I never stayed in touch. I don't really know. I bump into him from time to time in the street. He generally asks for cigarettes and money. I believe he's set himself up in some sort of detective agency.

REG A detective? Hmmm. How very interesting.

There is a strange thumping noise from upstairs. **REG** *starts violently, spilling tea everywhere.*

RICHARD Are you alright?

REG It's alright, I thought I heard, well, a noise that startled me. But it was nothing. Just overcome with the tea fumes, I expect. Let me just catch my breath. I think a little port will revive me excellently. So sorry, I didn't mean to startle you.

Waves in direction of port decanter, **RICHARD** *pours port into one of the three glasses.*

RICHARD What sort of noise?

Thumping heard again. There is, one hopes, a momentous air of Greek Tragedy about this. As though Clytemnestra is calling Agamemnon to tell him his bath's nice and warm.

REG That! *(Drops glass of port)* Did you hear that?

RICHARD Well, yes. Is there someone up there?

REG No. No-one. Nobody that should be there.

RICHARD Then…?

REG *(grave)* I must go up there. I must. Please wait for me here.

RICHARD Look, what is it? A burglar? Look, I'll go. I'm sure it's just the wind or something.

REG No, it is for me to do. Wait here.

Takes a few steps up stair, pauses, and turns round.

(Tragic hero tones) I am sorry that you have become involved, in what is… the more difficult side of my life. I do not know what awaits me up there, do not know exactly. I do not know if it is something which I have foolishly brought upon myself with my… my, my, hobbies, or if it is something to which I have fallen an innocent victim.

There is something that I must ask of you.

When I come back down these stairs, if my behaviour strikes you as being in any way odd, if I appear in any way not to be myself, then you must leap on me and wrestle me to the ground. Do you understand? You must prevent me from doing anything I may try to do.

RICHARD But how will I know? Sorry, I don't mean it to sound like that, but I don't know what…?

REG You will know. Now please wait for me.

REG *exits upstairs.* **RICHARD** *waits, incredulously. A door is opened, and the thumping sound, which is becoming, but is not quite yet, identifiable, is heard again. A little more time passes,* *and* **REG** *re-enters.* **RICHARD** *regards him warily, remembering his instructions.*

REG It's all right. It's just a horse in the bathroom.

    RICHARD *leaps on him and wrestles him to the ground. They fight. Elaborate as you like...*

    No, no. Get off me, let me go, I'm perfectly all right, let me go!

    They continue to tussle.

    It's just a horse, a perfectly ordinary horse, but, thank you for taking me at my word.

RICHARD A horse?

    They tussle some more.

REG Yes, four-legged thing with a big nose.

    They still struggle.

RICHARD A horse? *(He is lying down, pinned to the ground by* **REG** *who is panting a little)*

REG Yes, it is. Listen, I'm sorry if I... alarmed you earlier, it was just a slight turn. These things happen, don't upset yourself about it. Dear me, I've known odder things in my time. Far odder. She's only a horse, for heaven's sake. Let's have some port.

RICHARD But... how did it get in?

    REG *is pouring port as* **RICHARD** *gets up.*

REG Well, there was an open window, I expect she came in through that. Marvellous animals.

RICHARD You're doing it deliberately, aren't you?

REG Doing what, my dear fellow?

RICHARD I don't believe there's a horse in your bathroom. I don't know what you're doing. I don't know what any of this means, but I don't believe there's a horse in your bathroom.

    RICHARD *gets up, dusts himself off, and heads up the stairs.*

REG Poor fellow.

Sound of door opening, then loud dramatic whinny and other unmistakable horse noises.

There is a loud, pantomime toilet flush. **RICHARD** *re-enters. Shaken.*

RICHARD I agree. You do appear to have a horse in your bathroom, and I will, after all, have a little port.

REG *hands him some port.*

REG Just as well I put out three glasses after all. I wondered why earlier. Now I remember! You asked if you could bring your girlfriend but appear not to have done so after all. Never mind, these things happen.

RICHARD I did?

REG Oh yes, I remember now, you asked if it would be all right, I said I would be charmed and fully intended to be so. Maybe she decided that an evening with your old tutor would be blisteringly dull, and opted for the more exhilarating course of washing her hair instead. Dear me, I know I would have done. It's only the state of my hair that forces me to pursue such an active social round these days.

RICHARD Oh... my... god. Susan. I've forgotten again! I was supposed to pick her up, but I forgot. This is it. She's going to kill me. Reg, thank you so much, erm... I'm terribly sorry, but I have to run, I hope... the horse... erm... thanks...

He leaves hurriedly.

REG *sits himself down and sips quietly at his port. A neigh, not so violent this time, is heard.* **REG** *looks upwards fondly, rises, and fishing a carrot out of his coat pocket goes to feed his new friend.*

Scene Five

DIRK *appears, scanning the horizon with a pair of binoculars. As he does so a spotlight with a binocular-shaped filter scans the stage accordingly.*

Binoculars settle on the window of **SUSAN***'s apartment as* **RICHARD** *climbs in through it. He clearly doesn't have a clue what he is doing. Once inside the flat, he looks furtively around.* **DIRK** *produces a mobile phone and dials.*

SUSAN*'s landline rings.* **RICHARD** *dashes to the spot, picks up the phone.*

RICHARD Er, hello?

Then, realising what he has done, curses, drops phone, and then picks it up again.

DIRK Rule Number One in housebreaking. Never answer the phone when you're in the middle of a job. Who are you supposed to be, for heaven's sake?

RICHARD Who-who is this?

DIRK Rule Two. Preparation. Bring the right tools. Bring gloves. Try to have the faintest glimmering of an idea of what you're about before you start dangling from window ledges in the middle of the night. Rule Three. NEVER forget Rule Two.

RICHARD Who is this?

DIRK Just your neighbourly Neighbourhood Watch… If you'll just look out of the back window you'll see…

__RICHARD__ turns, __DIRK__ picks up a camera, and there is a flash.

Rule Four: never stand where you can be photographed. Rule Five… Are you listening to me, MacDuff?

RICHARD What? Yes… How do you know me?

DIRK Rule Five: NEVER admit to your name... I run a little course, if you're interested...

RICHARD *is silent.*

You're learning... slowly, but you're learning. If you were learning fast you would have put the phone down by now, of course, but you're curious – and incompetent – and so you don't. I don't run a course for novice burglars as it happens, tempting though the idea is. I'm sure there would be grants available. If we have to have them they might as well be trained. However, if I did run such a course, I would allow you to enrol for free, as I am curious to know why Richard MacDuff should have resorted to housebreaking. Stressful as software development is I wouldn't recommend cat burgling as occupational therapy.

RICHARD Who... are... you?

DIRK You are speaking with Dirk Gently, of Dirk Gently's Holistic Detective Agency.

RICHARD Dirk! What a... er, I mean...

DIRK Yes.

RICHARD Dirk – well, I mean, Dirk, how are you...erm – well, you know.

DIRK Richard, I bid you good evening. I would advise you to be at the Pizza Express in Baker Street in twenty minutes. Bring some money.

RICHARD Dirk...? Are you trying to blackmail me?

DIRK No you fool – for the pizzas.

(Click) Spot on **DIRK** *out. A key turns in the lock to* **SUSAN** *'s flat.*

RICHARD *hurriedly throws the phone down and runs to the sofa, trying to look relaxed.*

MICHAEL WENTON-WEAKES *(off) laughs nervously.*

SUSAN *(off: bored)* yes, Michael, well, of course you would. Are you coming in, then?

MICHAEL *(off)* That would be splendid.

SUSAN *enters, with* **MICHAEL**. *She switches light on.*

SUSAN Richard! *(She looks pleased to see him, then slaps him in the face)* I've been saving that up all evening, and don't try and pretend it's a bunch of flowers you've forgotten to bring that you're hiding behind your back, you tried that gag last time.

RICHARD It's a box of chocolates this time. I climbed up the entire outside wall without them. Did I feel a fool when I got in.

SUSAN Do you want something big and sharp thrown at you?

SUSAN ignores **RICHARD** *and speaks to* **MICHAEL**.

Oh Michael, don't just stand there like a slowly deflating pudding. Thank you very much for dinner. You were very sweet and I enjoyed listening to your troubles all evening because they were such a nice change from mine. But I think it would be best if I just gave you your book and pushed you out. I've got some serious jumping up and down to do, and I know how it upsets your sensibilities.

Exit **SUSAN** *to bedroom to get book.* **MICHAEL** *and* **RICHARD** *stare at each other awkwardly. Neither likes each other.*

RICHARD Michael...

MICHAEL Richard. I, er, read your piece in *Fathom*. On music, and, er... recycled algae?

RICHARD Recursive algorithms.

MICHAEL Yes of course. Very interesting. But, if you want my opinion, so wrong, so terribly wrong. For the magazine I mean. When I ran *Fathom* it was an arts magazine. That new editor has utterly ruined it. He'll have to go. Have to. Ross has no sensibilities and is a thief.

RICHARD He's not a thief, and you know it, Michael, nor did Ross have anything to do with you getting the push. When you "ran" *Fathom* it was a dismal failure masquerading as an excuse for expensive lunches. Gordon should have replaced you the minute he bought it. It was only because of your mother that he kept you on at all, and you can't deny that Al Ross has made it a great success.

MICHAEL Success? That's just it, Richard, you miss the point entirely – *Fathom* wasn't meant to be a success, it was mine, and that was the point of it. It wasn't about profit, money, or circulation figures. It reflected an older way of living. It was a forum for like-minded people, people sickened by the greed and waste of the modern pace of living. It was a bastion of...

Enter **SUSAN** *with book.*

SUSAN Now then children. Michael, here's your Coleridge back. *(She gives him the book and then ushers him out)* Thank you very much for a nice evening. Good night.

She kisses him good night, glaring at **RICHARD**.

MICHAEL, *over* **SUSAN***'s shoulder, makes a face at* **RICHARD**. *He leaves.*

RICHARD I suppose it would be pointless saying I'm sorry.

SUSAN Entirely.

RICHARD I'm really sorry. This time, I truly am. I know I said that last time.

SUSAN Do you remember last time?

RICHARD Yes, of course. Not really, no. No no, of course I do. That was... erm.

SUSAN Venice.

RICHARD Ah. Venice. Umm.

SUSAN Venice? The unbeatable romance of ruined palaces, the thrill of St Mark's, the haunting song of the Gondolier? The grinding tedium of Terminal 1 departure lounge? Surely you remember. No, that's right. You forgot.

RICHARD Yes, yes I did. Gordon called a meeting and I got distracted. You could have gone anyway...

SUSAN Not really. After eight hours at the airport, I'd drunk so much, they called security and a taxi.

RICHARD Susan, I'm sorry. It's just that I –

SUSAN Honestly Richard, you're just going to say you forgot again. How can you have the gall to stand here with two arms, two legs and a head, as if you were a human being? This is the behaviour that a bout of amoebic dysentery would be ashamed of. I bet that even the very lowest form of amoebic dysentery shows up to take its girlfriend out for a quick trot around the stomach lining once in a while.

RICHARD Susan, what can I say...

SUSAN You can say "ouch" for a start. You didn't even give me that satisfaction, and I thought I hit you rather hard.

RICHARD You did...

SUSAN God, it's freezing here. What's that window doing wide open?

She shuts it.

RICHARD Erm – I told you. That's how I got in.

SUSAN *turns round and stares at him.*

Really, like in the chocolate ads, only I forgot the box of chocolates.

SUSAN What on earth possessed you to do that? You could have been killed.

RICHARD Well, er, yes, I just wanted to be back here before you... it seemed the only way to... well, you took your key back, remember...?

SUSAN Yes, I got fed up with you coming and raiding my larder when you couldn't be bothered to do your own shopping. Richard, you really climbed up this wall?

RICHARD Well, I wanted to make sure I was here before you arrived. I pegged it all the way back from Cambridge, even got stopped for speeding.

SUSAN Well it would have been a good deal better if you were here before I left. *(She takes a set of keys from her pocket)* Here, if it's going to keep you alive. I'm too tired to be angry any more. An evening of being lobbied by Michael has taken it out of me.

The two are now sitting together on the sofa. To all intents and purposes, they are making up.

RICHARD I don't know why you put up with him. He's a spineless –

SUSAN I think you over-react. He's a man with ideas. Admittedly, he does have the personal charms of cat litter, but, if you scratch around a bit, you unearth some interesting things. It's a shame he and Gordon are such enemies, you know. They really ought to get on quite well. They're both hopeless obsessives with no communication skills.

Though I will have to steer clear of him if he keeps on going on at me about how Gordon sacked him from *Fathom*. For some reason Michael thinks I have some sway with Gordon. I'm just his baby sister.

To Gordon, I'm a utility. I keep you in line, keep Michael out of his hair, and I'm quite invaluable at important dinner parties when he remembers he hasn't got around to getting a wife yet.

RICHARD That's not true. Well, not entirely true.

SUSAN Talking of Gordon, I think I'd better turn down the volume on the answerphone. I have the horrible feeling a Gordon message is coming through, *(goes over to answerphone and turns volume down)* and I can't be bothered just now. I'll speak to him tomorrow. Just take the tape to the girl at the office tomorrow for me, would you? If there's anything important she can tell me. Oh, anyway, about the weekend – I'm afraid I have to work, sorry.

RICHARD *(relief)* I have to work as well.

SUSAN I know; Gordon keeps on at me to nag you. At least you don't do that. But I'm sure that there's some kind of grey area between being pressurised and being totally forgotten about that I'd quite like to explore. Give me a hug.

RICHARD Oh, I've promised to meet Dirk.

SUSAN Who?

RICHARD It doesn't matter, I'll see him tomorrow.

They kiss. Lights down.

Scene Six

Lights up on **GORDON**'s *car, a flashy convertible.* **GORDON** *is driving, the car hi-fi is playing* Bach's English Suite No.2 in A minor. *The music is in turn recorded by the answerphones of the various people* **GORDON** *calls in the course of this scene and is heard as a backdrop to his voice whenever the calls are replayed.*

GORDON *has just made a phone call. He has reached an answerphone.*

AL ROSS'S ANSWERPHONE. "This is Al Ross, Editor of *Fathom*. I'm not available right now. Please leave a message…"

GORDON Oh, Albert, hi – it's Gordon. Just on my way to the cottage. Bit misty on these roads. Listen, I have those people from the States coming down to the cottage over this weekend to thrash out the distribution and promotion strategies for *Fathom*, the marketing people from –

Sweeping head lights. Blaring horn.

Shit! That lorry had bright lights, none of these bastard lorry drivers ever dips them properly, it's a wonder I don't end up dead in a ditch. That would be something wouldn't it, leaving your famous last words on somebody's voicemail.

There's no reason why those lorries shouldn't have automatic light-activated dipper switches. I'll get Diane to send a letter from me to that fellow at the Department of the Environment saying we can provide the technology if he can provide the legislation.

What's the point in having a CBE if you can't kick a little ass?

(sighs) You can tell I've been talking to Americans all week.

SERGEANT GILKS *appears, he is reading from notes as though making a court appearance. He looks like, and indeed is, a plainclothes policeman.*

GILKS The weather forecast for the night in question was "changeable". A misty night, with poor visibility. Gordon Way was driving a grey Mercedes SLK. With the top down. Bastard. It appears that he'd always believed that "speed limits" were things that happened to other people.

GORDON That reminds me, God, I hope I've packed the shotguns. Why are the Americans always so mad to shoot my rabbits? I buy maps to persuade them to go on long, healthy walks, but they always end up shooting rabbits. I really feel quite sorry for the creatures. We should have one of those signs on the lawn like they have in Beverly Hills, saying "Armed Response." I'll have one made up with a sharp spike on the bottom at the right height for rabbits to see.

DIRK *appears at the opposite end of the stage to* **GILKS**.

He talks straight out to the audience.

DIRK Gordon Way's horoscope for the fateful night was almost as misleading as the weather forecasts. It mentioned an unusual amount of planetary activity in his sign and had urged him to differentiate between what he thought he wanted and what he actually needed, and suggested that he should tackle emotional and work problems with determination and complete honesty.

GORDON I got your message about Richard. I am sorry about him, but at least he misses your deadlines for articles as frequently as he misses mine for product launches. I'll talk to him in the morning.

GILKS It appears he was using his phone while driving. Very bad. Could get hurt that way.

GORDON And I hear that Michael Wenton-Weakes is up to his old tricks, again. Did he actually picket your office? All by himself? Unbelievable. What does he expect me to say? "Goodness me, Michael, this magazine is too successful, what I really want to do is make it crap and sell less copies – come back and edit it again!" He's starting to nag Susan as well. Either that or he fancies her – both probably. Perhaps we should have my post security-screened from now on, I wouldn't put it past Wenton-Weakes to courier me a melted rabbit. That reminds me, I've got to call Susan, I'll speak to you tomorrow, or I might call you back later, bye.

GORDON *ends call.*

GILKS The penultimate call from the subject's mobile phone was to a Mr Albert Ross, Editor of *Fathom* magazine and a Director of Way Forward Publishing, a subsidiary of Way Forward Technologies, or rather, the call was to his voicemail. Mr Ross was, like most sane people on a Friday night, out getting drunk. Sometimes it's the only way. After eighteen minutes, Mr. Gordon Way terminated that call and dialled his sister's home phone number.

GORDON *dials.* **SUSAN***'s answerphone answers.*

SUSAN'S MACHINE Hi, this is Susan Way, I'm not at home right now, but if you leave a message, I'll get back to you as soon as possible. Maybe.

GORDON Susan, hi, Gordon. It's Friday night, 1.47a.m., Saturday morning I suppose, you may be asleep, so I hope I get points for not calling your mobile phone. I'm about five minutes from the cottage, listen I don't like to ask you this sort of thing, but you know I always do anyway, so here it is – Richard and *Fathom*, Susan. Susan, *Fathom* and Richard. He's two articles behind. He says he'll get them done, but every time I see him he's got a picture of a sofa spinning on his computer screen. He says it's an important concept but all I see is furniture.

So can you, I don't like to ask you this, I really don't, but can you make him see how important it is? Just make sure he realises that Way Forward Technologies is an expanding commercial business, not a soft furnishings showroom...

GILKS That call was unexpectedly terminated.

GORDON Ah, here's the drive. That's odd, there's a noise coming from the boot. I thought I'd just closed it properly.

DIRK What both the weather forecast and the horoscope inexplicably failed to mention was that this was the last evening of Gordon Way's life.

DIRK, *with a bow to* **GILKS**, *exits.*

GORDON *gets out of the car. His boot springs open and a masked man appears. The figure lifts a shotgun and fires both barrels into* GORDON's *chest.*

GORDON *falls to the ground, there is very little doubt that he is dead.*

The figure sets to work on GORDON's *body. A maniacal laugh is a distinct possibility. Figure exits.*

GILKS   The body of Mr. Way was discovered in his car, which was parked in his driveway, just before dawn this morning. He had been shot, strangled, and then his car had been set on fire. The doctor who examined the body is of the opinion that Mr. Way was in fact strangled after he was shot, which seems to suggest a certain confusion in the mind of the killer. *(Exits)*

GORDON *gets up, dressed in a suit that would be immaculate if not for the large bloodstain on the shirt. He wanders past, dazed, muttering to himself. We can't hear what he's saying, but he appears to be pretty startled.*

He's even more shocked when he notices his body, especially when the killer returns and starts to pour petrol over it.

Out of instinct, GORDON *picks up his phone, and dials* SUSAN's *number again.*

SUSAN'S ANSWERMACHINE   Hi, this is Susan Way, I'm not at home right now, but if you leave a message, I'll get back to you as soon as possible. Maybe.

GORDON'S GHOST   Susan, Susan, help me! Help me for God's sake. Susan, I'm dead... I'm dead... I'm dead and... I don't know what to do. Help me, Susan... *(Beep)*

A phone rings, offstage, as this act ends and the next begins.

ACT TWO

Scene One

The offices of **DIRK GENTLY***'s Holistic Detective Agency.* **MISS JANICE PEARCE** *is at her desk, looking sullen. With a vicious black felt-tip she is drawing mustachios and spectacles on a magazine poster.* **DIRK** *is at his desk. Both desks have ringing phones on them.* **DIRK***, exasperated, answers his and the ringing stops.*

DIRK Hello, Dirk Gently's Holistic Detective Agency, how may we be of help to you? Yes Mrs. Sanderson, messy divorces are our particular speciality... er, no thank you, not quite that messy.

Puts phone down, hurriedly. **DIRK** *starts to study a newspaper (headline – "WAY SHOT," or something equally delicate). He stiffens. Picks up the phone and dials a single digit.* **JANICE***'s extension rings. She notices it, shoots him a glare through the open door, and steadfastly refuses to answer it. He gets up, and still with the phone under his ear, walks across to her desk.*

(*With his hand over the mouth-piece*) Miss Pearce!

JANICE *ignores him, and the phone, and concentrates on colouring in a pair of horns.*

Miss Pearce! The telephone is ringing. Could you please answer it?

JANICE, *with baleful glare, answers the phone.*

JANICE (*sigh*) Yes, Mr. Gently?

DIRK Ah, Janice (*into the phone, but glaring at her all the while, daring disobedience*) I'm expecting a client. A Mr. Richard MacDuff. When he comes, show him in.

JANICE *(equally defiant, also into the phone)* Shan't.

DIRK Why not? I insist that you show him in. That's what you're paid for.

JANICE You haven't paid me.

DIRK Nonsense Miss Pearce, I have paid you. I gave you a cheque only a week ago.

JANICE A cheque?! You cancelled it.

DIRK Ah, but only to save it from falling into the wrong hands.

JANICE Whose? My bank manager's?

DIRK One can never be too careful.

> **DIRK** *hangs up and plucks a large dictionary from a shelf and, walking across to her desk, hands it to* **JANICE**.

> This, Ms. Pearce, is a dictionary. I suggest you look up "secretary" in it, you may find a clearer understanding of your duties and responsibilities here than has hitherto been available to you.

> **JANICE** *accepts the dictionary. The phone rings again.* **JANICE** *reaches out as if to answer it, but then picks up a cigarette instead, and defiantly lights it.* **DIRK** *glares at her; she blows smoke in his face, spluttering he retreats to his desk to answer it, shooting a final shot:*

> You're fired.

JANICE I quit.

> *She slams open the dictionary and starts to tear pages out of it, sending paper aeroplanes whizzing into the audience as* **DIRK** *deals with the call.*

DIRK Dirk Gently's Holistic Detective Agency. Ah, Mrs. Sauskind, my oldest, and if I may say, most valued client. Good day to you Mrs. Sauskind, good day. Sadly, no sign as yet of young Roderick, I'm afraid, but the search for the noble cat is intensifying... ah yes, the bill, I was wondering if you had received it...

JANICE *remains at her desk, concentrating on tearing sheets out of* DIRK*'s dictionary.* DIRK *continues to mime phone conversation. Enter* RICHARD. *He sees her and blinks.*

RICHARD Is this the Detective Agency?

JANICE *frowns at him, and tears a few more sheets from the dictionary.*

And is Mr. Gently in?

JANICE *(tear)* He may be, and then again he may not be. *(Tear)* I am not in a position to tell. *(Tear)* It is not my business to know of his business. *(Tear)* His business is, as of now, entirely his own business *(Tear)*.

RICHARD Are you his secretary?

JANICE I am his ex-secretary, and intend to stay that way. If you'll excuse me, I'd like to storm out please. *(She slams the dictionary shut and passes it to* RICHARD*)*

She stands, grabs her bag, and walks out.

DIRK *(covering phone)* And good riddance.

The door slams. DIRK *beckons* RICHARD *in, but continues to talk to Mrs. Sauskind.*

Yes, Mrs. Sauskind, but I incline to the quantum mechanical view in this matter. My theory is that your cat is not lost, but that his waveform has temporarily collapsed and must be restored. Schrödinger, Planck and so on. *(To* RICHARD*)* Do you have any cigarettes?

RICHARD *pats his pockets and produces a pack of French cigarettes and offers one to* DIRK. *Pause.*

Oh no I couldn't possibly that would be most kind.

DIRK *swipes the packet, removes a cigarette, and places the packet in his pocket. He lights the cigarette.* RICHARD *is left agonised.*

(To phone) I believe, as you know, in the fundamental interconnectedness of all things. Furthermore, I have plotted and triangulated the vectors of the interconnectedness of all things and traced them to a certain beach in Bermuda, which

it is therefore necessary for me to visit from time to time in the course of my investigations.

Yes, expenses were well, expensive in the Bahamas, Mrs. Sauskind. It is in the nature of expenses to be so.

My dear Mrs. Sauskind let me say this. Do not worry yourself about this bill. Do not, I beg you, let it become a source of anxiety to you. Merely grit your teeth and pay it. As always, the very greatest of pleasures to speak with you, Mrs. Sauskind, for now, goodbye.

He hangs up. Gingerly.

My dear Richard MacDuff, welcome to my offices. *(Produces a pizza from underneath the desk)* Your pizza.

RICHARD What is this?

DIRK It is a Venetian Masterpiece. At least that's how the menu described it. I've told them you'll settle up when next you call in.

RICHARD No, what is this, all this? You appear to have a Holistic Detective Agency and I don't even know what one is.

DIRK I provide a unique service, at least in this world. The term "holistic" refers to my belief that what we are concerned with here is nothing less than the fundamental interconnectedness of all things.

RICHARD Yes, I got that bit earlier. It sounds like an excuse for exploiting gullible old ladies.

DIRK *lifts the lid and pulls out a slice of pizza.* **RICHARD** *makes to do the same, but* **DIRK** *snaps the box shut.*

DIRK Exploiting? Well, I suppose there would be if anybody ever paid me, but there never seems to be the remotest danger of that. I live in a chain of hope. I hope for fascinating and remunerative cases, my secretary hopes that I will pay her, her landlord hopes that she will produce some rent, the Electricity Board hopes that he will settle their bill, and so on. I find it a wonderfully optimistic way of life.

Meanwhile I give a lot of charming and silly old ladies something to be happily cross about and virtually guarantee the freedom of their cats. Is there a single case that exercises the tiniest part of my intellect, which, as you hardly need me to tell you, is prodigious? No. But do I despair? Am I downcast? *(The dramatic pause of a hero)* Yes. Until today.

RICHARD Dirk, I'm glad for you, but where does all that rubbish about cats and quantum mechanics come in?

DIRK I am sure, Richard, that you are familiar with the notion of Schrödinger's Cat.

RICHARD Yes. Why?

DIRK Explain it to me. Indulge me.

RICHARD *(slightly bored)* It demonstrates probabilistic behaviour at a quantum level at a macroscopic level. Or let us say an everyday level.

DIRK Yes, let's.

On screen: A cat appears. A box appears around the cat. Also in the box is a lurid green vial of poison gas, and a lump of radioactive material.

RICHARD Imagine that you take a cat and put it in a box. Also in the box you put a small lump of radioactive material, and a phial of poison gas. There is an exactly 50-50 chance that an atom in the radioactive lump will decay and emit an electron. If it does decay, then it releases the gas and kills the cat. If it doesn't, the cat lives. Fifty-fifty.

On screen: The box fills with gas, and the cat dies.

The point is, there's a rather extraordinary consequence. Until you do open the box, the cat exists in an indeterminate state. The possibility that it is alive and the possibility that it is dead are two different waveforms superimposed on each other inside the box. Schrödinger put forward this idea to show the absurdity of quantum theory.

On screen: The cat revives and looks annoyed.

DIRK Exactly. Bravo!

RICHARD But what's all that got to do with this, this Detective Agency?

DIRK Oh. That. Well, some researchers were once conducting such an experiment, but when they opened up the box, the cat was neither alive nor dead but completely missing. Understandably puzzled, they called me in to investigate, as someone who might not only have an eerie sympathy with cats, but also perhaps, an additional insight into the problems of quantum physics.

It was surprisingly simple. At a macroscopic level I was able to deduce that nothing very dramatic had happened. The cat had merely got fed up with being repeatedly locked up in a box and occasionally gassed and had taken the first opportunity to hoof it through the window. It was for me the work of a moment to set a saucer of milk by the window and call 'Bernice' in an enticing voice – the cat's name was Bernice, you understand – and the cat was soon restored. A simple enough matter, but it seemed to create quite an impression in certain circles, and soon one thing led to another as they do and it all culminated in the thriving career you see before you.

RICHARD Oh. And where do your remarkable psychic powers fit into this enterprise?

DIRK On that I maintain the same view that I have always held.

RICHARD Which is?

DIRK That I am not clairvoyant.

RICHARD Really? Then what about the exam papers?

DIRK *(with darkened eyes and in a low savage voice)* A coincidence, a strange and chilling coincidence, but nonetheless a coincidence. One, I might add, which caused me to spend a considerable amount of time in prison. Coincidences, I learned, can be frightening and dangerous things.

Coincidentally, if I may say so, having been watching you very carefully, you seem to be extremely relaxed for a man in your position.

RICHARD What are you talking about? Good heavens, Gordon hasn't got to you as well, has he?

DIRK Sorry? Got to me?

RICHARD Gordon, Gordon Way. He's always pressurising people into trying to get me to work. No. No I'm just getting paranoid. So... um, what?

DIRK The famous Gordon Way <u>has</u> this habit, has he?

RICHARD Yes, I don't like it. Why?

DIRK I think you'd better sit down, though this may not come as a shock. *(Tosses paper at* **RICHARD***)* The body of Gordon Way was discovered before dawn this morning. The nature of his death was both brutal and bizarre.

RICHARD Oh God. Oh God. *(Stands)* I must phone Susan.

DIRK Mr. Richard MacDuff is one of the two people most likely to benefit from Mr. Way's death, since Way Forward Technologies would almost certainly pass at least partly into his hands. The other person is the same Miss Susan Way whose flat Mr. MacDuff was observed to break into last night. The police don't know that bit of course, and nor, if we can help it, will they.

RICHARD *sits down.*

DIRK *pulls down the blind.*

However, any interaction between the two of them will naturally come under close scrutiny.

DIRK *produces a metronome, with a silver tea-spoon strapped to the hand, and sets it ticking.* **RICHARD***, already in shock, begins to fall under* **DIRK***'s spell.*

The news reports on the radio say that they are urgently seeking Mr. MacDuff, who they believe will be able to help them with their inquiries, but the tone of voice says that he's clearly guilty as hell.

DIRK*'s melodious voice paces itself as he stands and slowly swoops over the prone* **RICHARD***.*

I charge two thousand pounds a day, plus expenses. Expenses are not negotiable and will sometimes strike those who do not understand these matters as somewhat tangential. They are all necessary, and are, as I say, not negotiable. *(Eyeball to glazed eyeball)* Am I hired?

Scene Two

The driveway of **GORDON***'s country cottage. His car is still there, as is his dead body.*

On screen: A flashbulb pops, the picture of **GORDON***'s dead face.*

GORDON'S GHOST *watches, shocked, as his body is zipped up into a body bag by* **PERKINS**, *an ugly policeman.* **GILKS** *is interrogating* **GORDON'S HOUSEKEEPER.** *The* **HOUSEKEEPER** *is elderly and befuddled. She gives a little squeak of fear at seeing the policeman examining her employer's body.*

GILKS Sorry ma'am – it must be a very unpleasant sight for you. Perkins – scarper! *(***PERKINS** *leaves, dropping* **GORDON** *with a thunk)* Sorry about Perkins, ma'am – ugliest man on the force. We all have nightmares about him – last thing I see at night, whenever I shut my eyelids. His face – it's imprinted there. He's always worse after a full moon.

HOUSEKEEPER Why?

GILKS Oh, you'd have to ask his mother about that. Perkins doesn't like to talk about it... Anyway, you were telling me about your employer, the late Mr Way.

HOUSEKEEPER Well, Sergeant Gilks, he just liked to talk, really. Often I could leave the Hoover for ten minutes and make myself a cup of tea and he'd still be talking when I got back. I never liked to leave it longer than that – fifteen minutes and the Hoover would have walked away, too.

GILKS And you saw nothing suspicious last night? Nothing that struck you as in any way odd?

HOUSEKEEPER No, like I said, I left him his supper, in case he came back from the office, and then went home. I saw nothing odd.

GILKS Just for the sake of argument, if I were suddenly to do this... *(he pulls a bizarre face, sticks his tongue out and dances up and down,* *twisting his fingers in his ears)* would anything strike you about that?

HOUSEKEEPER Well, yes. I would think you had gone stark raving mad.

GILKS Good, it's just that some people have a different idea of what odd means, you see. If last night was an ordinary night just like any other night, then I am a pimple on the bottom of the Marquis of Queensbury. The late Marquis of Queensbury. We shall be requiring a statement later. Perkins!

PERKINS *re-enters. The* **HOUSEKEEPER** *gives a shriek of fright as he leads her away.*

This is all very bizarre...

PERKINS *re-enters and resumes his work.* **GILKS** *stands still centre stage, as* **GORDON**'s *house fades away. Lights gradually up on* **SUSAN**'s *flat, with* **SUSAN** *sitting stunned on her sofa.* **GILKS** *is now obviously mid-conversation with her.*

...and must be something of a shock.

SUSAN You could put it that way.

GILKS Can I get you –

SUSAN I'm fine thanks. I hate tea, and I think I've only got sherry in the house.

GILKS *(producing a hip-flask)* I was going to offer you some of this.

SUSAN That's much better. *(Swigs – pulls face)* No it isn't. Please don't tell me you confiscated this from a tramp. How did my brother die?

GILKS He was shot getting out of his car early this morning. With both barrels – so it's not suicide.

SUSAN Don't be so sure with Gordon – he was very thorough.

GILKS We have one of his computers down the station, you know.

SUSAN Really?

GILKS Yes. Buggered if we can get it to work.

SUSAN Which model is it?

GILKS I think it's called a Quark II.

SUSAN Oh well that's simple. It doesn't work – never did. Gordon always called it a heap of crap.

GILKS Funny thing, that's what I've always said.

SUSAN *(fondly)* It was hopeless – it was one of the reasons why Gordon's first firm went bust. I suggest you use it as a paperweight. They're rather good at that.

GILKS Oh, I can't do that Miss Way. The door would keep blowing open.

SUSAN What do you mean, officer?

GILKS I use it to keep the door closed. Nasty draughts down the station this time of year. In the summer, of course, we beat suspects round the head with it. *(Looks at notebook)*

SUSAN Of course. I'm sometimes tempted to hit Richard with mine.

GILKS Mr MacDuff?

SUSAN Yes – my boyfriend. He's worked for Gordon since the start.

GILKS We know that. Do you happen to know where he was last night at the time of your brother's death?

SUSAN Yes, yes he was with me.

GILKS 'He was with his girlfriend at the time of the murder.' Lovely. I've never heard that one before. And, ah, where is Mr MacDuff now?

SUSAN I don't know, exactly. He said something about seeing an old friend, Dirk, something...

GILKS *(choking with surprise)* Gently!

Scene Three

Phone ringing. Lights gradually up. DIRK*'s office.* JANICE *is back, smoking astride the desk.*

JANICE   Good afternoon, Wainwright's Fruit Emporium. Mr. Wainwright is not able to take calls at the moment since he thinks he is a root vegetable. Thank you for calling.

Lights up over this to show DIRK*'s office.* RICHARD *slumped in hypnosis.*

JANICE *has just slammed down the phone and is emptying her desk and listening to the door.* RICHARD *comes round.*

DIRK   Please do not disappoint me by saying "Where am I?" A vacant glance will suffice.

RICHARD *gazes vacantly.*

A fascinating evening you appear to have spent, even though the most interesting aspects of it seem to have escaped your curiosity entirely.

RICHARD *looks dazed.* DIRK *wanders into the outer office.*

You've been under hypnosis for over an hour, during which time I've learnt many useful things, and been puzzled by a good many others. Yet, we have some interesting threads to pull on. For, of everything you have told me, only one thing is actually impossible.

RICHARD   Impossible?

DIRK   Yes, completely and utterly impossible. Luckily, you have come to exactly the right place with your impossibility.

RICHARD   Impossible?

DIRK   Everything about it. Completely and utterly – well, let us say inexplicable – there is no point in using the word impossible to describe something that has clearly happened. Even if it cannot be explained by anything we know. And anyway, there is no such word as impossible in my dictionary. In fact, *(holds up dictionary)* everything between "herring" and "marmalade" appears to be missing.

RICHARD What can't be explained by anything we know?

DIRK Well, for a start the professor's conjuring trick with the salt cellar in the pot.

RICHARD That? It's only a conjuring trick – sleight of hand – he does them all the time. I'm sure if you asked any conjurer, he would say it's easy once you know how. I once saw a man in New York doing –

DIRK I know how these things are done. *(He opens the pizza box. A live rabbit is revealed.* **DIRK** *lifts it into a drawer)* These things, you see, are easy. Sawing a lady in half is easy. Joining her together again is less easy but can be done with practice. The trick you described to me with the pot is... completely and utterly inexplicable.

RICHARD Oh, there was probably some detail of it I missed.

DIRK Undoubtedly, but the benefit of questioning you under hypnosis is that it allows me to see the scene in much greater detail than even you were aware of at the time. You see, take the little girl. Do you recall what she was wearing?

RICHARD Erm, no. A dress of some kind I suppose – it was dark, she was a bit away from me and I was hardly...

DIRK She was wearing a dark blue, cotton velvet dress gathered to a dropped waist. It had raglan sleeves gathered to the cuffs, a white Peter Pan collar, oh, and six small pearl buttons down the front. The third one down had a small thread hanging off it. She had long, dark hair pulled back in a red butterfly hair clip. You told me yourself under hypnosis.

On screen: Surveillance pictures of the little girl with diagrammatic cutaways of her clothes flash up over this narration.

RICHARD No, no. I don't even know what a Peter Pan collar is.

DIRK Ah, but I do. And you described it perfectly. As you did the conjuring trick, and that trick was not possible in the form in which it occurred. There are some questions I would like answered about the professor, and about the note that you discovered. There is an answer for which I would like the question. I refer of course to the questions asked by George III. And then, perhaps there's that horse...

RICHARD Dirk! Dirk! I'm about to be arrested for murder and you're telling me about pots, ponies and Peter Pan collars. I don't think any of it has the remotest connection with Gordon's death –

DIRK But I do believe that they are connected.

RICHARD That's absurd.

DIRK Along with anyone who follows quantum mechanics to their logical extent I cannot help but believe that all things are fundamentally connected. But I also believe that some things are a good deal more interconnected than others. And when an impossible event followed by a whole string of highly peculiar ones happens to a person who becomes the suspect in a bizarre murder, then it seems to me that we should look for the solution in the connection between these events. You are the connection, and you yourself have been behaving in a highly peculiar manner.

RICHARD No, I have not.

DIRK You climbed the outside of a three-storey building and broke into your girlfriend's flat.

RICHARD It may have been unusual, it may have been unwise, but it was perfectly logical. I needed to get there before she did. I wanted to make up for letting her down; I needed to make everything right again...

DIRK Not at all irrational then? Nothing really out of the ordinary? So, you are perfectly satisfied with your actions and your reasons for doing them? It's what anyone would have done?

RICHARD I don't say anyone would have done it. I probably have a slightly more logical turn of mind than many people, which is why I can write good code.

DIRK Uh-huh. Do you know what my old maiden aunt who lived in Winnipeg used to tell me?

RICHARD No. No, I don't.

RICHARD *reacts strangely to* **DIRK***'s mention of his maiden (starts suddenly, and then, moving slightly jerkily as if in a trance, he proceeds to perform an extravagant musical number, with as many other cast members as possible joining in. The specifics of the musical number do not matter. What does matter is that it is (a) completely unexpected (b) performed with genuine gusto and aplomb. At the end of the number, all except* **DIRK** *and* **RICHARD** *exit,* **RICHARD** *shakes himself out of his trance and sits looking a little dazed...*

DIRK Do you often do that?

RICHARD No, not often. I just find that music relaxes me a little.

DIRK And that was why you did it?

RICHARD Well yes, I just thought it would help me deal with all this. Good job you had that piano *(or such other musical instrument or prop as was actually used)* there.

DIRK Not a little disproportionate, then, to stop what you were doing and pretend to play the piano, even though I haven't got one.

RICHARD You haven't?

DIRK You're satisfied with your reasons?

DIRK *produces a dictaphone and lets it play.*

DIRK'S VOICE You will forget all this, except for the instructions I am about to give you. When you hear me mention my old maiden aunt who comes from Winnipeg *(restrains* **RICHARD***)*, you will immediately leave what you are doing and perform an extravagant musical number.

RICHARD *is shocked.*

DIRK I would be interested to know what made you climb into Susan's flat last night, and why.

RICHARD Susan gave me the tape from her answerphone. The tape's in my flat. I picked it up. Dirk, I'm suddenly very frightened by all this.

JANICE's *phone rings, she answers it sotto voce. Blackout, save for spot on* **JANICE**, *on the telephone.*

JANICE Hello – you've reached Professor Planck's physics laboratory. I'm afraid the professor can't come to the phone right now, because I've just locked him in the particle accelerator, and he's hurtling towards uncertain death at near light speed...

Scene Four

RICHARD's *flat. It is split over two floors – a main entrance and living area and an upstairs study filled with computers. A staircase, partially blocked by a sofa, connects the two.*

On screen: the slowly rotating sofa.

PERKINS *stands on guard. He is holding a hacksaw, and making trial saws at the air.* **DIRK** *sweeps on looking official.*

PERKINS Excuse me, Sir –

DIRK You – the sofa in the stairwell. Guard it. Do not let anyone touch it, and I mean anyone. Understood?

PERKINS I've had orders to saw it up.

DIRK Countermanded. Watch it like a hawk. Stay here. Do not let anyone pass, and I mean, anyone. Understood?

PERKINS Yes sir.

DIRK *(points to waste bin)* Have you searched that?

PERKINS Er yes –

DIRK Search it again. Keep searching it. Who's here?

PERKINS Er, well –

DIRK I haven't got all day.

PERKINS Sergeant Gilks just left, with –

DIRK Good. Gilks is off the case. I'll be in here if I'm wanted, but I don't want any interruptions unless it's very important. Understood?

PERKINS Er, who –

DIRK I don't see you searching the waste paper basket.

PERKINS Er, right sir. I'll –

DIRK I want it deep-searched. You understand?

PERKINS Er –

DIRK Get cracking.

> **DIRK** *sweeps past him, up into* **RICHARD***'s study. He produces a magnifying glass and starts to burn ants with it, whilst fiddling with the computer and looking for the answerphone machine.*

> **SERGEANT GILKS** *enters, takes one look at the waste paper basket, clips the policeman smartly over the head and bellows up into the gallery.*

GILKS Dirk Gently! When I discover a police officer dismembering an innocent waste paper basket I have to ask myself certain questions. And I have to ask them with the disquieting sense that I am not going to like the answers. I had a horrible premonition, Dirk Gently, a very horrible premonition indeed. A premonition, I might add, that I now find horribly justified. I don't suppose you can shed any light on a horse discovered in a bathroom as well? That seemed to have an air of you about it...

DIRK No, but it interests me strangely. (**DIRK** *finds the answerphone tape*)

GILKS I should hope it bloody did, especially if you had to take the bloody thing downstairs at one o' clock in the bloody morning... What the hell are you doing here?

DIRK Why Sergeant Gilks, I am here in pursuit of justice.

GILKS Well, wouldn't mix with me then. *(Turns momentarily away)* What do you know of MacDuff and Way?

DIRK I hear they have a "Greatest Hits" album due soon. *(Pockets tape)* Oh, that MacDuff and Way. Of Way I knew nothing beyond common knowledge. MacDuff I knew at Cambridge.

GILKS Oh, you did, did you? Describe him.

DIRK Tall and absurdly thin. And good-natured. A bit like a preying mantis that doesn't prey – a non-preying mantis if you will. A sort of genial mantis that's given up preying and taken up tennis instead. And of course, completely incapable of murder.

GILKS That's for us to decide. Is he your client?

DIRK He is.

GILKS All right Gently, where is he?

DIRK I haven't the faintest idea.

GILKS I'll bet you've got a billing address.

> **DIRK** *shrugs, charmingly.*

Look Gently, this is a perfectly normal, harmless murder enquiry, and I don't want you mucking it up. So consider yourself warned off as of now. If I see a single piece of evidence being levitated I'll hit you so hard you won't know if it's tomorrow or Thursday. Now get out, and give me that tape on your way.

DIRK *(genuinely surprised)* What tape?

GILKS Look Gently, just because you think you're bloody clever doesn't mean that everybody else is stupid. If I turn away it's for a reason, and the reason was to see what you picked up. I didn't need to see you pick it up, I just had to see what was missing afterwards. We are trained, you know. We used to get half an hour Observation Training on Tuesday afternoons. Just as a break from four hours solid Senseless Brutality.

> **DIRK** *produces tape with a sigh.*

Now put that tape back in the machine, and play it. Let's see what you didn't want us to hear.

DIRK It wasn't that I didn't want you to hear it. I just wanted to hear it first.

> **DIRK** *puts tape in answering machine.*

GILKS So do you want to give us a little introduction?

DIRK It's a tape from Susan Way's answering machine. Way apparently had this habit of leaving long answerphone messages on people's landlines...

GILKS Yeah, I know all that. What's the point?

DIRK Well, I believe there may be a message on the tape from Gordon Way last night.

GILKS I see. OK. Play it.

The tape plays. As it does, **GORDON**, *dressed entirely in white, enters, near* **GILKS**. *He mouths along to the message. He is shot (on the tape), and jerks back.* **DIRK** *stops the tape.*

One minute twenty seconds since he said it was one forty-seven. Stay here. Don't move. Don't touch anything. I've made a note of every particle of air in this room, so I shall know if you've been breathing. Bodie, get on to Way's office. Doyle, get the details of Way's mobile phone, what number, which network...

He exits. **GORDON** *looks distraught at* **GILKS**' *exit, then focuses his attention on* **DIRK**.

GORDON Excuse me, I say, excuse me. Look I know you can't hear me – but I think you might be the only one who can help me. The thing is – the thing you've got to help me with, is that I'm not actually gone yet. I mean, I'm dead, but I'm not gone – and I think I need your help.

DIRK *continues to poke around the room, quite oblivious to* **GORDON**'s *entreaties.*

Look, it's Dirk, isn't it? Richard mentioned you a number of times. Said you had some sort of psychic thing going on? Never really set any store by that sort of paranormal rot before. Before I became a ghost, that is. All seems slightly more reasonable now that I look at it, from the other side, as it were. Hmmm. Perhaps I am going about this the wrong way. Think like a ghost, Gordon, think like a ghost, how would a proper ghost do this?

GORDON's *manner changes. He jumps astride a desk behind* **DIRK** *and proclaims theatrically:*

Hear me now, Dirk Gently – I am thy client's boss's ghost! Listen to the tape!

DIRK *(suddenly conscious of* **GORDON**'s *presence, but imprecisely)* If anyone can hear me, hear this. My mind is my centre and everything that happens there is my responsibility. Other people may believe what it pleases them to believe, but I will do nothing until I know the reason why and know it clearly. If you want something then let me know, but do not dare touch my mind.

GORDON *sighs and deflates.* **DIRK** *presses play.*

ANSWERPHONE Next message, received 1.54 a.m.

GORDON'S RECORDED GHOST VOICE Susan, Susan, help me! Help me for God's sake. Susan, I'm dead... I'm dead... I'm dead and... I don't know what to do.

GORDON *looks expectant, hoping that* **DIRK** *will now be able to help him.* **DIRK** *presses stop on answerphone, and looks around the room, trying to pinpoint the location of the disturbance. He chooses a point, it happens to be the right one, so his next lines are directed precisely at* **GORDON**.

DIRK I'm sorry but I have the welfare of my client to consider. If this tape is to establish the time of Gordon Way's death, then I don't want any embarrassing examples of Gordon speaking to turn up on it after that point – even if they are only to confirm that he is in fact dead.

DIRK *hits 'erase' on the answerphone.*

ANSWERPHONE Message – erased

GORDON No!

Discordant howling sound effect as **GORDON** *runs around the room using new found poltergeist powers to fling books and furniture, mostly into the gallery at* **DIRK**. **GILKS** *enters.*

GILKS I'm going to come in again, and when I do, I don't want to see anything of this kind going on whatsoever. Understood?

He leaves.

DIRK I don't know who you are, but I can guess. If you want my help, don't ever embarrass me like that again! Now, go!

GORDON *scowls at* **DIRK**, *and stops throwing the furniture. He storms off, kicking the waste bin and* **GILKS** *comes back on.*

GILKS *(re-enters and surveys mess)* Ah, there you are. I'll pretend I can't see any of this, so that I won't have to ask any questions the answers to which would, I know, only irritate me. What's that tape doing?

DIRK Rewinding.

GILKS Hmmp. Your client is cleared. The call was placed at 1.47a.m., over two hours after Mr. MacDuff was stopped for speeding, and at a time when your client was, according to Mr. Way's sister, with her. The porter of Miss Way's apartment block, who was on duty all night witnessed Mr. MacDuff leave Miss Way's apartment early this morning. As to why they didn't answer the phone during this time –

DIRK What would men such as us know of young love, Gilks, what could we know?

GILKS Hmmmp.

Scene Five

DIRK's *offices.* **JANICE** *is sorting out the mail. Phone rings.*

JANICE *(answering phone)* Hello, Madam Delilah's massage parlour, how may we service you?

DIRK *is pacing furiously, brows furrowed with concentration.* **JANICE** *enters the inner office with a stack of bills.*

There's a letter from the Inland Revenue...

DIRK No, please – there are wilder skies than these.

He goes to his desk and picks up a large sheet of paper, which is covered in blue felt-tip squiggle, and gives it to **JANICE** *who looks at it in bemusement.*

What do you think?

JANICE It looks like a lot of meaningless squiggles done in blue felt-tip on a piece of typing paper. It looks like you did them yourself.

DIRK No! Well, yes, but only because I believe that it is the answer to the problem!

JANICE What problem?

DIRK The problem of the impossible conjuring trick!

JANICE Couldn't have been impossible or he wouldn't have done it. Stands to reason.

DIRK Exactly! Exactly! Consider this. An intractable problem. Clearly I wasn't going to be able to think of anything else until I had the answer, but equally clearly I would have to think of something else if I were ever going to get the answer. How to break this circle? How to look the ineffable squarely in the eye and manage to eff it after all? Ask me how.

JANICE How?

DIRK By writing down what the answer is! And here it is! I have transformed the problem from an intractably difficult and possibly insoluble conundrum into a mere linguistic puzzle. Albeit, an intractably difficult and possibly insoluble one. Go on; say that it's insane – but that it just might work!

He makes a grand, sweeping exit. **JANICE** *remains behind, shaking her head sadly.*

JANICE It's insane, trust me.

Scene Six

SUSAN's *flat.* **SUSAN** *is playing the cello* (Bach's Suite No 2 in D minor for unaccompanied cello). **RICHARD** *enters.* **SUSAN** *throws him a wan smile but keeps playing until she comes to the end of the prelude. There is a fierce intensity to her playing, as if all her emotions and grief are being channelled into the piece.*

There is a plate of pickled herrings and other half-eaten lunch things on the table.

SUSAN Sorry, I didn't want to stop. How are you?

RICHARD *(shrugs)* You?

SUSAN Pretty shitty. Better for that *(the music)*, but still I can hardly even think. It's just so awful. I'm glad you're here now. Gordon was just so present in life, it's hard to get used to the idea of his absence… Ironic, isn't it. You, me, we're the ones who loved him most and we spent our time avoiding him… *(shrugs, sighs)* Look, have some lunch, then we can talk. Except, I don't really want to talk about Gordon for a while – not with you, not with anyone… not until it all sinks in.

SUSAN *gets up and fiddles with the lunch things…*

Work keeps my mind off it. It would have been easier if we'd been somehow closer, but I wasn't and I feel embarrassed by not really having some more profound reaction to it all. Talking about it would be all right, except that you have to use the past tense and that's what…

RICHARD *gets up and hugs her.* **SUSAN**'s *landline rings. Enter* **GORDON** *with the* **GHOST** *of his mobile phone.* **SUSAN** *picks up her phone.*

GORDON Susan! Susan! Can you hear me! Susan I'm still here, I'm a ghost and I'm not alone… I need…

SUSAN *hangs up.*

SUSAN Nobody there. That's happened a couple of times. I think it's some sort of minimalist heavy breather. They don't even try to sell me anything. Now, what's all this about you being wanted by the police?

RICHARD Well, in connection with Gordon, I mean I must be a suspect.

SUSAN A suspect? You – oh Richard don't be absurd, no one thinks you did it. They want to question you of course, but –

RICHARD And they're not out searching for me?

SUSAN No! Where on earth did you get that idea from?

RICHARD Er, well, this friend of mine told me.

SUSAN Which friend?

RICHARD His name is Dirk Gently.

SUSAN Who is he? You've never mentioned him. Did he say anything else?

RICHARD He runs a detective agency. A holistic one. And he hypnotised me, and made me perform a rather ambitious musical number. And er, that's about it really.

SUSAN Richard. I'm glad you came over. At first I thought I needed to see you, but now I think you need to see me.

Security phone buzzes, **SUSAN** *gets it.*

Who? Oh. I see. You'd better come in. Your friend, Mr. Gently.

DIRK *bursts in.*

DIRK Miss Way *(kisses her hand)* it is the most inexpressible pleasure to meet you, but also a matter of the deepest regret that the occasion of our meeting should be one of such great sorrow, and one that bids me extend to you my most profound sympathy and commiseration. I ask you to believe me that I would not intrude upon your private grief for all the world, if it were not on a matter of the gravest moment and magnitude. Richard – I have solved the problem of the conjuring trick, and it is extraordinary.

He sits.

RICHARD You'll have to excuse us Dirk –

DIRK No, I'm afraid you will have to excuse me. The puzzle is solved. "What, then, is the solution?" you ask me. Or rather you would if you could get a word in edgeways, which you can't, so I will save you the bother and ask the question for you, and answer it as well, by saying that I will not tell you, because you won't believe me.

SUSAN Believe me, I won't.

DIRK Instead I shall show you this very afternoon. It explains everything – the trick, the note you found. THAT should have made it perfectly clear to me but I was a fool – and it explains what the missing third question was, or rather, I should say, the first!

RICHARD What missing third question?

DIRK The missing question that George III asked of course! Ha!

RICHARD Asked who?

DIRK Don't you listen to anything you say? The whole thing was obvious. So obvious that the only thing that prevented me from seeing the solution was the trifling fact that it was completely impossible. Sherlock Holmes observed that once you have eliminated the impossible, then whatever remains, however improbable, must be the answer. I however, refuse to eliminate the impossible. Now, let us go.

SUSAN Go where?

DIRK Miss Way, the police are only interested in knowing who murdered your brother. I, with the very greatest respect, am not. I wanted to know, still desperately need to know why Richard climbed into this flat last night.

RICHARD I told you why.

DIRK What you told me is immaterial – it only reveals the crucial fact that you do not know the reason yourself! A fact which has led me, using my intellect alone, to uncover possibly the greatest secret lying hidden on this planet. I swear to you that this is true and that I can prove it. Richard MacDuff, if you were not quite yourself when you climbed the wall last night... then – who were you and why?

RICHARD What does this have to do with conjuring tricks?

DIRK That is what we must go to Cambridge to find out. Come Richard. What are those?

He's noticed the plate of pickled herrings.

SUSAN Pickled herrings. Would you like one?

DIRK Thank you no. There is… no such word as "herring" in my dictionary. Good afternoon, Miss Way, wish us God speed.

INTERVAL

ACT THREE

SCENE ONE
The Story So Far Scene

There are two halves to this scene – **DIRK**'s *monologue, followed by a bonus on-screen recap. They should be played back to back, but in the absence of a screen and film, just using the first is fine.*

Enter **DIRK**. *He is drinking from a saucer of milk and chewing on a realistic, dead mouse. He pauses, holds it away from him contemplatively, and then throws it into the audience. He lights a cigarette and addresses the audience.*

DIRK You may have wondered why I called you all here today. The fact is that one of us in this room is a murderer!

Let us examine the story so far. By 'story' I of course mean this series of seemingly random events that are in fact fundamentally interconnected and germane to the very structure of what we laughingly term existence.

Fact! Gordon Way has been murdered.

Fact! A number of people stand to profit from his death. Shall we list just some of the suspects?

Could it be dashing, maverick Editor Al Ross? Spurned publisher Michael Wenton-Weakes? Gordon's sister, Susan? Baffled employee Richard MacDuff? The enigmatically confused Professor Chronotis? A maniacal hitchhiker? Perhaps maybe we should look further afield…

Fact! Richard MacDuff has been proved, by me, to have been hypnotically influenced by something or someone – but to what foul purpose?

Fact! Professor Chronotis is worried about several things, not least the horse in his bathroom.

Could the solution to all these problems be somehow related to the sofa that is impossibly stuck on Richard's stairs? Or a simple magical trick, that, despite requiring a woolly hat is completely and utterly impossible?

Brace yourselves for impact, because you can be certain that the fate of everyone in this theatre hangs in the balance. Farewell.

He stands, stubbing the cigarette in the saucer and exits.

(Voice over) And now the same information for our transatlantic friends.

On screen: The explosion and then the screen shows the **DIRK** *logo, while some dramatic music plays, reminiscent of a Star Trek cliff-hanger.*

VOICE OVER *(gravely American tones)* Previously on Dirk Gently, Vampire Detective...

Gunshots.

GORDON'S VOICE *(American accent)* Susan! Susan! Help me Susan, I'm dead!

A car screeches. There is the sound of a car crash and more explosions.

VOICE OVER Following the murder of his employer, dashing young programmer Richard MacDuff must turn to the forces of darkness to aid his quest for vengeance.

DIRK'S VOICE *(American growl)* Welcome to the offices of Dirk Gently's Holistic Detective Agency. This is your pizza.

More explosions and a siren. A woman screams.

VOICE OVER In a world where brutal murder is just a symptom of a far darker mystery, a mystery that threatens the entire existence of the human race. In a race against time, humanity's last, best hope is the truth...

DIRK'S VOICE There is no such word as impossible in my dictionary.

More gunfire. A crescendo of an explosion.

VOICE OVER And now, the continuation...

Scene Two

REG's *study.* **RICHARD** *and* **DIRK** *enter across the stage.* **DIRK** *has obviously mistaken himself for a tour guide.*

DIRK St. Cedd's, the college of Coleridge, and the college of Sir Isaac Newton, renowned inventor of the milled edge coin and the cat flap.

RICHARD The what?

DIRK The cat flap! A device of the utmost cunning, perspicuity and invention. It is a door within a door, you see, a...

RICHARD Yes, there was also the small matter of gravity.

DIRK Gravity, yes, there was that as well, I suppose. Though that, of course was merely a discovery. It was there to be discovered. *(He takes a coin and tosses it into the audience)* You see? They even keep it on at weekends. Someone was bound to notice sooner or later. But the cat flap... ah, there is a very different matter. Invention: pure, creative invention.

RICHARD I would have thought it was quite obvious. Anyone could have thought of it.

DIRK Ah, it is a rare mind indeed that can render the hitherto non-existent blindingly obvious. This, if I am not mistaken is the door we seek. Shall we enter?

DIRK *knocks and they enters.* **REG** *is in the kitchen.*

REG *(off)* Come in!

(off) Sit down, whoever you are. I'm just making some tea.

DIRK That would be most kind. We are two.

They sit.

REG Indian or China?

DIRK Indian, please.

REG Milk?

DIRK Please.

REG One lump or two?

DIRK One please, and two spoons of sugar if you would.

REG pops his head round door.

REG Dirk Gently! Good heavens! Well that was quick work, young MacDuff, well done. My dear fellow, how very excellent to see you, how good of you to come. My dear, dear Dirk. *(Handshaking)*

DIRK How have you been then, my dear Professor?

REG Well, it's been an interesting time recently, or rather, a dull time, but dull for interesting reasons. Now sit down again. I will get the tea and then endeavour to explain. *(Exits to kitchen)*

RICHARD I had no idea you knew him so well.

DIRK I don't. We met once by chance at some dinner, but there was an immediate sympathy and rapport.

RICHARD So how come you never met again?

DIRK He avoided me, of course. Close rapports with people are dangerous things if you have a secret to hide. And as secrets go, I fancy this one is something of a biggy.

Enter **REG**.

REG Did I ask if you wanted any tea?

RICHARD Er, yes… we spoke about it at length. I think we decided in the end that we would, didn't we?

REG Good. By a happy chance there seems to be some ready in the kitchen. You'll have to forgive me. I have a memory like a… like a… what are those things you drain rice in? What am I talking about?

REG makes puzzled exit.

DIRK Very interesting. I wondered if his memory might be poor. *(Examines room, notices abacus)* Is this the table where you found the note about the salt cellar?

RICHARD Yes, tucked into a book on Greek pottery.

DIRK Yes, yes, of course. We know about all that. I'm just interested that this was the table.

REG *(roar from off-stage)* Sieve! That's what I've got a memory like!

RICHARD Well, it's an odd coincidence that the book should have been...

DIRK Coincidence! Hah! We shall see how much of a coincidence and we shall see exactly how odd it was. I would like you, Richard, to ask our friend how he performed the conjuring trick.

RICHARD I thought you said you knew.

DIRK I do. I would like to hear it confirmed.

RICHARD Oh, I see, that rather easy isn't it? Get him to explain it, and then say, "Yes, that's exactly what I thought it was!" Very good Dirk. Have we come all the way up here in order to have him explain how he did a conjuring trick?

DIRK Please do as I ask. You saw him do the trick, and you must ask him how he did it.

Enter **REG** *with tea.*

Professor Chronotis.

REG Reg, Please.

DIRK Very well, Reg. I must tell you that I know your secret.

REG Ha, yes, er, do you indeed? I see. Yes I was afraid of that.

DIRK And there are some questions we would like to ask you. I must tell you that I await the answers with the very greatest apprehension.

REG Indeed, well, perhaps it is, at last, time. I hardly know what to make of recent events. Very well, ask what you will.

DIRK *nods at* **RICHARD**.

RICHARD Er... well, I'll be interested to know how you did the conjuring trick with the salt cellar last night.

REG The conjuring trick?

RICHARD Er, yes, the conjuring trick. How the salt cellar got inside the pot.

REG Oh, well, that's perfectly straightforward, didn't take any conjuring skill at all. I nipped out for my hat, remember?

RICHARD Yes.

REG Well, while I was out of the room, I went to find the man who made the pot. Took some time of course. About three weeks of detective work to track him down, and another couple of days to sober him up, and then after a little difficulty I persuaded him to bake the salt cellar into the pot for me. I had to time my return a little carefully so as to make it all look perfectly natural. I bumped into myself in the anteroom, which I always find embarrassing; I never know where to look. But, er, there you have it. Apart from the horse, of course – that must have just wandered in while I was in Greece. These things happen when you leave the door on the latch...

RICHARD What on earth are you talking about?

REG I thought you said you knew my secret.

DIRK I do. He as yet does not, although he furnished all the information I needed to discover it. Let me fill in a couple of blanks.

In order to help disguise the fact that you had in fact been away for weeks, when as far as anyone sitting at the table was concerned, you had only popped out of the door for a couple of seconds, you had to write down the last thing you said, in order to be able to pick up the thread of conversation again. An important detail if your memory is not quite what it once was.

REG What it once was... I can hardly remember what it once was. But yes, you are very sharp to pick up such a detail.

DIRK And then there is the little matter of the three questions King George III asked. Asked you. He asked you if there was any particular reason why one thing happened after another, and if there was any way of stopping it. Did he not also ask you, and ask you first if it was possible to move backwards in time, or something of that kind?

REG I was right about you. You have a very remarkable mind, young man. Yes, yes, that is precisely what he said.

DIRK Good, then that explains why the answers were Yes, No and Maybe, in that order.

On screen:
Q: Is it possible to move back in time?
A: Yes.

Q: Is there any particular reason for one thing happening after another?
A: No.

Q: Is there anyway of stopping it?
A: Maybe.

Now, where is it?

REG Where is what?

DIRK The time machine.

REG You're standing in it.

Dramatic chord. **DIRK** *checks the soles of his shoes.*

Scene Three

MICHAEL *on stage, alone. He is talking to someone, who is not quite himself.*

MICHAEL I've lost everything, you see. Once, once before all this began I had it all. A father, a magazine, and a way of life I understood.

Then one day, my father tried to change a plug on a lamp. It was an ugly little lamp – I still have it upstairs on the window sill. The only thing about it which is worthy of attention is that it is the lamp that electrocuted my father.

The old boy was such a fool with anything electrical. I can still see him, peering with profound concentration through his half moons and sucking his moustache as he tried to unravel the arcane complexities of the thirteen amp plug. Having mended the lamp, he had, it seems, plugged it back in without first screwing the cover back on. Only then did he try to change the fuse. From this he received the shock that stilled his already dicky heart.

All this time my mother had been patiently waiting in the wings. With my father's death, she'd been let loose, and now everyone was running for cover.

Some people describe my mother as an old battle-axe, that's quite unfair. If my mother is a battle-axe it's not old, but antique; an exquisitely crafted, beautifully balanced battle-axe, with an elegant minimum of engraving that stops just short of its gleaming, razor sharp edge. One swipe from such a weapon, and you wouldn't even know you'd been hit until you tried to look at your watch a bit later and discovered your arm wasn't on.

My father was more than happy for *Fathom* to be an institution – a highly respected, if not exactly profitable, magazine. And of course it gave me something to lunch about. My mother wasn't quite so content. It took her only minutes to realise that I had been... how shall we say, anecdotalising the revenue figures... And then she asked to see me.

He acts out his mother's voice.

– Ah, Michael. There you are. How do you want me to treat you – as my son or as the Editor of one of my magazines? I'm happy to do either.

– I am your son, but I don't see...

– Right. Michael, I want you to look at these figures. The ones on the left show the actual incomings of your little magazine. The figures on the right show your own notion of the incomings. Does anything strike you about them?

– Mother, I can explain, I –

– Good, Well, that's all perfectly satisfactory, then.

– Don't you want to hear?

– No that's all right, dear, I'm sure the new owner of *Fathom* will be glad to listen to whatever it is.

– The new owner? What? You mean you're actually selling *Fathom?*

– No. I mean I've already sold it. Didn't get much for it, I'm afraid. One pound, plus a promise that you would be retained as Editor for the next three issues.

– But...

– Well, come now, we could hardly continue under the present arrangement, could we? We always agreed that the job shouldn't be a sinecure for you. And since I have a great deal of trouble either believing or resisting your stories, I thought I'd hand the problem on to someone more objective. Now, I have another appointment.

– Well, but... who have you sold it to?

She smiled. Up until now her lips had been tight. Not pursed, just thin and determined. "Gordon Way" she said.

– Gordon Way! But for heaven's sake, Mother, he's –

– Very anxious to patronise the arts. He's already secured quite a coup for *Fathom* – he's got Albert Ross to help you out. I'm sure you'll get on splendidly, dear. Now, if you don't mind...

– Mother, I've never heard anything so outrageous!

– Do you know, that's exactly what Mr Way said when I showed him these figures and then asked that you be kept on as Editor for the next three issues.

– But Mother... what difference would it have made to all this if I'd said treat me as the Editor of one of your magazines?

– Why dear, I should have called you Mr Wenton-Weakes, of course. And I wouldn't now be telling you to straighten your tie.

He straightens his tie.

SCENE FOUR

REG's study. As we left it.

RICHARD Who are you?

REG I have absolutely no idea. Much of my memory is gone completely. I am quite startlingly old, you see. I've seen an awful lot, you know. Forgotten most of it, thank God. Trouble is, when you start getting to my age, which, as I think I mentioned earlier, is a somewhat startling one – did I say that?

RICHARD Yes, you did mention it.

REG Good. I'd forgotten whether I had or not. The thing is that your memory doesn't actually get any bigger, and a lot of stuff just falls out. So you see, the major difference between someone of my age and someone of yours is not how much I know, but how much I've forgotten. And after a while you even forget what it is you've forgotten, and after that you even forget that there was something to remember. Then you tend to forget, er, what it was you were talking about...

RICHARD Things you remember...?

REG Smells and earrings.

DIRK I beg your pardon?

REG Those are things that linger for some reason. The earrings that Queen Victoria wore on her Silver Jubilee. Quite startling objects. Toned down in the pictures of the period, of course. The smell of the streets before there were cars in them. Hard to say which was worse. That's why Cleopatra remains so vividly in the memory, of course. A quite devastating combination of earrings and smell. I think that will probably be the last thing that remains when all else has finally fled. I shall sit alone in a darkened room, *sans* teeth, *sans* eyes, *sans* taste *sans* everything but a little grey old head. And in that little grey old head a peculiar vision of hideous blue and gold dangling things flashing in the light, and the smell of sweat, cat food and death. I wonder what I shall make of it all.

RICHARD How long have you been here?

REG Here? Just about 200 years. Ever since I retired.

DIRK Retired? From what?

REG Search me; I can't remember a thing. Must have been something pretty good though, what do you think?

RICHARD You mean you've been here, in the same set of rooms, for 200 years and nobody said anything? You'd think somebody would have noticed...

REG Oh, that's one of the delights of the older Cambridge colleges, everyone is so discreet. If we all went about mentioning what was odd about each other we'd be here till Christmas. *(DIRK reaches for the abacus)* Dirk, my dear fellow, please don't touch that at the moment.

DIRK What is it?

REG Why, it's exactly what it looks like, an old wooden abacus. I'll show you it in a moment. But I must congratulate you on your remarkable powers of perception. May I ask you how you arrived at the solution?

DIRK I have to admit that I did not. In the end I asked a child. I told him the story of the conjuring trick, and asked him how he thought it had been done, and he said, "It's effin' obvious, innit, he must have had an 'effin' time machine." He then kicked me rather sharply on the shin, and my only contribution could be to see that he was right.

REG But you had the perception to think of asking a child. Very well then, I congratulate you on that instead.

DIRK How... does it work?

REG Well, it's terribly simple really, it works any way you want it to. I simply plonk my abacus down there and it understands what I want it to do. I think I must have been brought up to use an abacus when I was a... well a child, I suppose. It's quite fun really, in its own way. Certainly better than television, and a great deal easier to use than a DVR. If I miss a programme I just pop back in time and watch it. I'm hopeless fiddling with all those buttons.

DIRK You have a time machine and you use it for... watching television?

REG Well, I wouldn't use it at all if I could get the hang of all these damned electrical boxes. It's a very delicate business, time travel, you see. Full of the most appalling traps and hazards. If you changed the wrong thing you could disrupt the entire course of history. Plus of course, it mucks up the telephone. Every time I use the time machine, which is hardly ever at all, partly because of this very problem with the phone, the phone goes haywire and I have to get some lout from the phone company in to fix it – and then he starts to ask stupid questions, the answers to which he has not the least hope of understanding. Anyway, the point is that I have a very strict rule that I must not change anything in the past at all – whatever the temptation.

DIRK But you broke your own rule last night! You changed something in the past!

REG Yes, but that was different. Very different, if you had seen the look on that poor child's face. So miserable. She thought the world should be a marvellous place and all those grizzled old dons were pouring withering scorn on her, just because the world wasn't wonderful for them anymore. No, that was perfectly justifiable, otherwise I make it a very strict rule...

RICHARD Reg, may I give you a little advice?

REG Yes of course my dear fellow, I should adore you to.

RICHARD If our mutual friend here should offer to hypnotise you, don't let him.

REG Whatever do you mean?

DIRK He means that he thinks there may be something a little disproportionate between what you actually did, and your stated reasons for doing it.

REG Oh. He has a very odd way of saying it.

DIRK Well, he's a very odd fellow. But you see, there may be other reasons for your actions which you may not be aware of. As in the case of post-hypnotic suggestion – or possession.

REG Possession?

DIRK Professor, I believe there was some reason you wanted to see me. What exactly was it?

Scene Five

*A wedding party, in full regalia, cross from stage left to stage right. The bride is radiant, the groom dashing, music plays, small children scatter rose petals etc. One guest (***AL ROSS***), in the rear of the procession, stops to tie his shoelace. As the rest of the party exits stage right, a mysterious tall stranger, dressed in oil-skins and carrying a crossbow enters – ominously. As he lowers his hood, we see it is* **MICHAEL WENTON-WEAKES**, *but not as we know him. Commanding of brow, domineering in stature, mad as a hat.*

MICHAEL Albert Ross?

ROSS *(not looking up, still intent on his lace)* Yes, yes.

MICHAEL You are a guest at this wedding?

ROSS *(looking up)* Why, yes, of course. Michael? Michael Wenton-Weakes is that you?

MICHAEL Yes. And yet, it is more than I. I, and also another. One known to you, Albert Ross, known of old.

ROSS Well, yes. Right, well we should be getting on now, eh, don't want to miss the champagne. I didn't realise you knew Malory or Alex? Er... er...

ROSS *isn't dumb and it's dawned on him that something is seriously wrong here. He makes as if to get away,* **MICHAEL** *restrains him with a look. Church bells sound.*

MICHAEL *(chuckling madly)* "The wedding guest he beat his breast", eh, Ross? But you cannot choose but hear! One wedding guest, One ancient mariner, One glittering eye, One cross bow *(he cocks the crossbow and aims it squarely at* **ROSS***)*, One Albert Ross. I think we know how this one is going to pan out, don't we?

ROSS *turns as if to run, his face a mask of horror.* **MICHAEL** *starts to launch manically as we black out. The high pitched whine of a crossbow bolt flying through the air is heard, then a thunk and a scream, and then the silence.*

Scene Six

REG You remember, when you arrived this afternoon, I said that times recently had been dull, but for... interesting reasons?

DIRK & RICHARD Yes?

REG Well, the truth is that for many weeks, months even, I have not used the time machine at all, because I had the oddest feeling that someone or something was trying to make me use it. It's not the first time. It comes on every few centuries. It's extremely disturbing and I had to fight it very hard, as I am, as I said strict about the use of time. As soon as I began to realise that it was something else trying to invade me, things got really bad and the furniture began to fly about.

RICHARD Is that what you were afraid of last night, upstairs?

REG Oh yes, most terribly afraid. But it was only that rather nice horse which, as I said, must have wandered in while I was in Greece.

DIRK Rather a complex business wasn't it? You're satisfied with your reasons for doing it?

REG It was worth it. Cheering up a little girl, so charming and delightful. You should have seen her; you'd have done the same thing; except of course for all that trouble with the telephone. Nothing's ever that easy is it?

DIRK No. No.

REG *(bothered)* It was a fairly major operation in temporal engineering, now that I face up to it. Much easier to compliment her on her dress, or something. Maybe the... ghost, we are talking of a ghost here aren't we?

DIRK I think we are, yes.

RICHARD A ghost? Now come on...

DIRK Wait! Please continue...

REG It's possible that the ghost caught me off my guard.

DIRK And now?

REG Oh, it's gone completely. The ghost left me last night.

DIRK And where, we wonder, did it go next? *(Stares at* **RICHARD***)*

RICHARD No please. Not this. I'm not even sure I've agreed about time machines yet, and now it's ghosts?

DIRK So what made you risk death by scaling a three-storey building? What made the professor go back in time for a pot? We have a ghost that wants something done and is looking for the right person to do it. I believe that hypnosis and possession work in very, very similar ways. You can be made to do all kinds of absurd things, and will then cheerfully invent the most transparent explanations. But – you cannot be made to do something against the fundamental grain of your character. You will fight; you will resist!

REG I'm afraid he's right. I see now I've always been too much of a struggle for the ghost.

RICHARD Now hold on, I have yet to be convinced that there is not some other explanation than that of ghosts to...

DIRK Richard, if it looks like a duck and quacks like a duck, we have at least to consider the possibility that we have a small aquatic bird of the family *Anatidae* on our hands.

RICHARD Then what is a ghost?

DIRK I think that a ghost is someone who died with unfinished business on his, her, or its hands. Who cannot rest until it has been finished or put right. Which is why a time machine would have such a fascination for a ghost.

It will be back. It tried first to take possession of Reg himself, but he resisted. Then came the incident with the conjuring trick, the pot, and the horse in the bathroom. Just as it was all getting a little complicated, you appear on the scene.

The ghost deserts Reg and concentrates instead on you. There occurs an odd but significant incident – you realise that you had made a mistake in the past – you had left Susan stranded. The ghost seizes its chance – will you change the mistake you had made, to make up for it, to undo it, just to see if it was in your character. But then, the ghost abandons you in turn – it must have found someone else. Someone even easier. Who? Who?

RICHARD Dirk, this is no time for owl impersonations. *(***DIRK** *glares him down, and* **RICHARD***'s scepticism collapses)* I felt the ghost leave me... when Michael Wenton-Weakes walked out of the room.

DIRK I wonder what possibilities the ghost saw in him?

There is a knock at the door. Enter **MICHAEL WENTON-WEAKES.**
He is carrying a bag.

MICHAEL I have come... for your help...

Dramatic chord.

Blackout.

Scene Seven

SUSAN's *flat.* **SUSAN** *is playing the cello –* Bach's Suite No 3 in C Major for solo cello. (BWV 1009.) **GORDON** *is holding his mobile phone. He dials.*

SUSAN *looks at the phone in annoyance, but continues playing.*

SUSAN'S MACHINE Hello, this is Susan. There's a movement that Bach wrote just to annoy cellists, so I can't come to the phone at the moment. *(Beep)*

GORDON Susan, thank God you're not listening, well I wish you were there, but the annoying thing about being a ghost is that you can only talk to answering machines. Pretty bloody ironic, huh? Susan, well, I suppose you've worked it out by now, but I'm dead. God, that sounded stupid – for the first time in my, well, life, I feel a bit sheepish about talking to these things.

God, I hate them. No, sorry. Look, this will probably be the last time I can talk to you and I want to get it right. There's so much to say. But perhaps you already know most of it. I hope so. Do you remember when you were ill, and Mum thought you might have…

The music rises in volume and intensity. **GORDON** *continues to talk but we can no longer hear him. We can though see the love in his face as he watches his sister, and listens to her play. Perhaps he plays with her hair, perhaps he just listens and sees her as she is – a strong young woman, a sister any big brother, even an egotistical undead one, would be proud of.*

…so. That's what I wanted to say. And now, I've got to go. Goodbye, sis. Goodbye, Susan.

The answerphone beeps.

SUSAN, *distracted by the noise, stops playing.*

MACHINE You have one message. *(Click)*

GORDON *smiles and turns away.*

Scene Eight

REG*'s study.* MICHAEL *stands before* REG, RICHARD *and* DIRK. *He looks very possessed indeed. You certainly wouldn't sit near him on the Tube.*

MICHAEL *(to* REG *and* RICHARD*)* I realise I owe you both an apology, and I only hope that as you come to understand my desperation, and the hope which your time machine offers me, you will understand, and forgive me. And help me. I beg you.

DIRK Give the man a whisky.

REG Haven't got any whisky. Er... port? There's a bottle of Margaux I could open. Very fine one, should breathe for an hour, but I could do that of course, it's very easy I –

MICHAEL Will you help me?

DIRK Why have you possessed the body of this man?

MICHAEL I need to have a voice with which to speak and a body with which to act. No harm will come to him, no harm...

DIRK I ask again. Why have you taken over the body of *this* man?

MICHAEL He was willing, both of these two gentlemen quite understandably resisted being... hypnotised; your analogy is fair. This one? His sense of self was at a low ebb, and he has acquiesced to my presence. I am very grateful and will not do him any harm.

DIRK His sense of self was at a low ebb...

RICHARD Yes I think that's probably true. He seemed very depressed last night. The one thing that was important to him had been taken away because he, well, he wasn't really very good at it. I suppose at least he feels wanted.

DIRK Hmmn. Hmmmmm. Hmmmmm. Michael Wenton-Weakes!

MICHAEL *(suddenly in his normal voice)* Yes?

DIRK You can hear me, and you can answer for yourself?

MICHAEL Oh yes, most certainly I can.

DIRK This being, this spirit. You know he is in you? You accept his presence? You are a willing party to what he wishes to do?

MICHAEL That is correct. I was much moved by his account of himself, and am very willing to help him. In fact I think it is right for me to do so.

DIRK All right. You can go. *(Snaps fingers)*

MICHAEL *slumps back into possession.*

All right. Now tell me your story again. And this time don't even try to make me feel sorry for you, so from now on leave out all that poetry...

RICHARD Coleridge! It sounded exactly like Coleridge! *Rime of the Ancient Mariner*!

DIRK Coleridge?

MICHAEL I tried to tell him my story. I –

DIRK You'll have to excuse me, I've never cross-examined a four-billion year old ghost before. Are we talking Coleridge, poet here? Are you saying you told your story to Samuel Taylor Coleridge?

MICHAEL Yes, I tried to tell him my story, I was able to enter his mind at certain times – when he was in an impressionable state. I told him my story, but unfortunately he was so... relaxed...

REG When he was on laudanum? I sometimes encountered him when he was quite astoundingly relaxed.

MICHAEL ...it became somewhat garbled, and what he wrote was not entirely accurate.

REG Poetic licence, me dear fellow. Besides he had to make it believable. Even so, it was the most God-awful epic poem. Dreadful, long turgid thing about ice-maidens, star voyages, and pleasure domes. Volumes of the wretched stuff. What was it called? *Fubli Fun? Genghis San?*

DIRK *Kubla Khan?*

RICHARD What are you all talking about? Kubla Khan isn't an epic poem at all – it's only seventy-three lines long, an unfinished fragment. According to an essay I never wrote, he was just settling down to write it when he was distracted by a man from Porlock. That was three hundred years ago. What does it have to do with your conjuring trick anyway?

REG *(chortling)* Oh, dear it all comes back to me now, I'm not the man I was, thank goodness. Mind you, I don't think I ever was the man I was.

DIRK What did you do?

REG Well, the original version of *Kubla Khan* just rambled on for hundreds and hundreds of lines. Terrible, turgid stuff. It threatened to ruin the reputation of the college. Common Room was in uproar. Something had to be done. The most awful self-pitying psychedelic poppycock. It had to go I'm afraid. The honour of the college was at stake.

MICHAEL *(anguish)* What did you do?

REG Well, I had to prevent the garbage from ever being written, so I nipped back in time to when Coleridge was writing the thing; put on a false beard, knocked on his door, said I was from a nearby village, and had a merry little chat with him about this and that. He looked most annoyed, blithered on about this poem he had a mind to write. Soon put a stop to that – thank goodness. Work of a moment really. And it just shows how any work of literature can be improved by judicious cuts.

(to **MICHAEL***)* Sorry, old chap but it looks like I'm the only being in this timeline who's read your biography. Still, couldn't put it down if that's any consolation. Gripping stuff. I'll make some coffee. *(Exits)*

RICHARD It's another world.

DIRK *(to* **MICHAEL***)* But enough remained, didn't it? There are enough traces of your story in his poems to influence people.

MICHAEL At times, like the Coleridge dinner. But not often. I've been loitering around this college for years. Waiting. And before there was even a college. I've been waiting.

REG *(head through hatch)* Around since the start of the university? Dear me, why haven't they made you chancellor yet…? Surely an oversight…

MICHAEL I have waited for so long. Watching. Helping. We were on a ship, a spaceship you see. We were on a journey. Our old world was consumed by violence and war. We were determined to make a new start, to achieve our ultimate aim...

DIRK Which was?

MICHAEL Well, to found a new and better world on which we could all live in freedom, peace and harmony forever, of course.

DIRK Oh, that. You thought this out carefully, I gather.

MICHAEL But we crash-landed on your planet before we arrived at our final destination. The damage was severe. As ship's engineer, I was given the task of overseeing repairs.

DIRK What went wrong?

MICHAEL I made the fatal mistake of relying on the automated service drones to carry out the repairs. They too had been damaged, and I only realised how severely when it was too late. As we started up the engines, the craft exploded and we were all destroyed. All for one simple mistake. A small connection that was never made.

DIRK So? What happened next?

MICHAEL Since then I have been alone on this planet. Alone, with the knowledge of what I had done. Alone, alone, all, all...

DIRK Yes, skip all that. What did you do?

MICHAEL I stalked the world, alone, for billions of years. It is impossible for you to conceive of even the tiniest part of the torment of such eternity. Then, life arose on this planet. Vegetation, things in the sea, then, at last, you. And I had to watch it happen all over again. The wars, the horrors, the steady, creeping decay. I've been watching for so long.

Enter **REG** *with coffee.*

REG So what do you want us to do?

MICHAEL Take me back, I beg you. With your machine. Take me back to the ship. A word from me and the repairs can be made, the launch aborted. This whole mistake ended. I will cease to be a burden to you.

REG So you would like me to use my time machine. To take you back into the past and change it?

MICHAEL I have waited four billion years. *(Smiles, like a charming haddock)* I will even say "please".

RICHARD But that can't work, can it? If we do that, then this won't have happened. Don't we generate all sorts of paradoxes? Changes?

REG Hmm. No major ones. No worse than many that exist already. The universe is rather like a human body. A few cuts and bruises here and there don't hurt. Time and space heal themselves up soon enough and people simply remember a version of events that makes as much sense as possible.

DIRK Are you sure? No real side effects?

REG A few things will seem a trifle odd, but if you've got through life without that already happening to you, then I don't know which universe you've been living in, but it isn't this one. It was all so long ago. There was no life around to be affected.

MICHAEL You... have my word on that.

RICHARD I think we should help him.

REG I agree.

MICHAEL My thanks...

DIRK I don't like it. Not one bit.

REG Splendid. Help yourself to cream. *(Rubs hands)* I think we ought to press on. There's no time like the present is there? It, ah, may be an idea to hold your cups quite firmly.

REG *plays with the abacus, and a howling wind arises.*

There are sounds – a roaring TARDIS, the Ride of the Valkyries, and a chiming clock. Stacks of books spin and whirl and the room dissolves in spinning furniture and smoke.

On screen: Spinning clocks, whirling and merging, their hands wheeling out of control. Shots of clouds moving across the sky, merging into an endless tunnel of time. Briefly, a police box hurtles into view, and then is lost from sight.

REG *seems intent on trying to pass around the sugar bowl.*
MICHAEL, **RICHARD** *and* **DIRK** *are hurled around the room.*

DIRK So this is time travel?

REG Yes, fun, isn't it? Rather like taking a stroll in a particularly bracing wind. *(Hands around plate)* Ginger snap anyone?

MICHAEL *(stands against the wind)* The roaring wind! it roar'd far off,

It did not come anear;

But with its sound it shook the sails

That were so thin and sere.

With my crossbow I shot the albatross!

He throws back his head and bays with satanic laughter. Bless him.

Scene Nine

REG's study. As the lights creep up there is the sound of a cup of tea being stirred. REG is sitting calmly by his abacus, sipping tea. The others are scattered. There is no sign of MICHAEL.

On screen: prehistoric landscape.

REG Prehistoric Earth.

The others begin to stir. **DIRK**, *rubbing himself, sets off for the exit.*

I wouldn't go out there. The air is poisonous. I don't know what it is, but it would certainly get your carpets nice and clean.

RICHARD Where are we?

REG Bermuda. It's a bit complicated.

DIRK And where is your hitchhiker?

REG In the bathroom. Changing.

DIRK Oh.

MUSIC: Thus Spake Zarathustra

MICHAEL *enters at the top of the stairs, in silhouette, in full scuba costume. Ridiculous. He waddles down the steps. The others line up to greet him. He performs a ceremonial wave with his flippers. He shakes hands.* **DIRK** *scowls.*

Well, then, be off with you. Good riddance. I wash my hands of the whole affair. I suppose we'll have to wait here for you to send back the empty, for what it's worth.

REG My dear fellow, consider what a very small effort it is for us to help the poor soul. I'm sorry if it seems to you an anti-climax after all your extraordinary feats of deduction. I know you feel that a mere errand of mercy is not enough for you, but you should be more charitable.

DIRK Charitable. Hah! I pay my taxes – ish—what more do you want?

Sulks on the sofa.

MICHAEL Well, thank you Professor Chronotis. My people shall... always be in your debt.

(He bows, gravely) Goodbye. *(He waves in an odd circular motion, three times)*

DIRK Now, what on earth did that mean? *(DIRK imitates wave)*

RICHARD Still looking for something to puzzle over? Something else to challenge your remarkable skills of reasoning?

DIRK I'm actually waiting for a phone call.

RICHARD What? Dirk, why can't you just face it that there's just a very simple, if impossible, explanation to everything. That ghost seemed like a perfectly reasonable, persuasive man.

REG I agree.

DIRK Professor, why are you so eager to help something you have been fighting for centuries to avoid? Both of you are yet again disguising an awkward truth with a lot of woolly fabrications. There is something we have all been overlooking.

The phone rings. (If possible, this is a duck phone, and so it quacks.)

Ah, hah! This will be for me...

REG I extremely doubt it. I refuse to believe that the one time the phone works is when we are four billion years in the past. I wonder if it's some bizarre new service like call waiting...

DIRK *(picking up phone)* Hello?

Enter **GILKS**, *holding a crossbow and a mobile phone.*

GILKS Ah, Gently, is that you? Your secretary told me I could find you here. Well, she told me I could find a "fat, self-deluding bastard" on this number, which, I quickly deduced, meant you. Where the hell are you when I need you?

DIRK Bermuda.

GILKS Bermuda! Christ, there's no way I'm claiming that back! Listen, Gently, it's bad. Susan Way's in hysterics. Says she's received some sort of message on her answerphone from Gordon Way saying he's dead. She was incoherent and kept babbling. We'd have ignored it as a hoax only it contained one very disturbing piece of information. One that proved to be correct. Albert Ross, the Editor of *Fathom*, is dead. Murdered. Shot with a crossbow at a friend's wedding. Apparently MacDuff owed him an article.

DIRK MacDuff has an alibi, I can assure you.

GILKS I'm sure he has, Gently, but not one we can't beat out of him. And we will, unless you can tell me where Michael Wenton-Weakes is.

DIRK Oddly enough I can. He's just gone to thumb a lift.

GILKS If you ask me, Gently, the toad's as guilty as hell.

DIRK My dear Sergeant Gilks, I am inclined to agree with you. And now, if you will excuse me, I have to prevent him from committing genocide.

GILKS What? But...

DIRK Don't worry, Sergeant, my bill is in the post.

Replaces phone. Quickly.

As you may have heard, Sergeant Gilks has just told me some very interesting things. Namely that Michael Wenton-Weakes went to a wedding, and, with a crossbow, shot Albert Ross.

There is an embarrassed pause.

RICHARD Dirk, that sounds like the ramblings of a drugged lunatic.

REG Of course it did. It sounded like that damn Coleridge.

DIRK Precisely. The key was murder. Wenton-Weakes, your little orphan there, has just killed Gordon Way and Ross. And he's gone out there to kill again.

RICHARD I don't understand.

DIRK The ghost tested everyone it took over, but found no subject that could commit anything against their own character. No host was prepared to commit murder. Until Michael Wenton-Weakes.

RICHARD Wait a minute! Why did the ghost want a murderer?

DIRK Because he thinks we've supplanted them. Humanity is an error. This was where they were going to settle and build their blasted paradise. On this dead planet. Without life. Out there, amongst all those noxious chemicals is a lot of goo and gook waiting on a massive dose of radiation to become life. He needs someone prepared to go out there and reverse all that – whatever the cost.

I would not be surprised to discover that the explosion your poor tormented soul out there is trying to reverse is the very thing that started life on this planet!

RICHARD What?

REG Oh good heavens.

DIRK The explosion will set into motion the evolution of life. Random amino acids will be catalysed into spontaneously forming DNA chains, these will grow, mutate and evolve. You're the scientist – work it out. From the goo – you.

RICHARD This isn't just another conjuring trick is it?

DIRK Michael Wenton-Weakes has gone out there to destroy civilisation as we know it. *(Dramatic chord)* I have, as you can guess, always wanted to say that.

REG You are right. Ohhhhh dear.

DIRK We're running out of time... wait a minute...

RICHARD Wait? Wait? There isn't time.

DIRK Richard, this is a time machine. We have all the time in the world...

REG Yes, but how much is that?

DIRK All we want! Professor *(he gestures towards the abacus)* do you not see? We now have a chance to employ your time machine to end this once and for always...

REG *(enthusing)* To ride the light fantastic...

RICHARD What?

DIRK Take us back to just before he left. And then hold us there – in that instant of time –

RICHARD You mean create a bubble of stasis in the space-time continuum; using the time machine as a trans-dimensional sub-particular buffer embolism... *(he's very excited)*

DIRK I thought you didn't believe in time machines?

RICHARD I didn't – until it quacked. Like a duck.

DIRK Can you do it Professor?

REG Ooh, I don't know. Sounds fiddly. I've never tried it before.

DIRK We have to prevent him from preventing us.

REG Well, I suppose it should be possible to take the time machine on a short journey into its own past. That would bring the ghost back here and hold him while his spaceship explodes. But it's tricky. Tricky. You're not supposed to meddle around with internal time frames. The maths are a fright, it will probably ruin my relationship with British Telecom permanently, and then there's the whole issue of temporal mass – when you try and move a time machine's future into a its own past it increases exponentially – it's rather like trying to park a lorry inside a Ford Cortina. And don't even get me started on the Blinovitch Limitation Effect...

RICHARD Yes, but can't you just reverse the polarity of the neutron flow through the flux capacitor?

REG My dear boy, it's only a bloody abacus. But, yes, I will try. What have we got to lose? If it doesn't work we'll never know since we'll never have existed anyway. *(He beams, pleased with this. Then his face falls, as he realises the full implications)*

The professor picks up his abacus and begins to play. The tea things whirl around the room. There is smoke, and flashing lights.

On screen: The time tunnel appears again, but warped and twisted. Odd, alarmed objects shift through our field of vision – rubber ducks, double decker buses, a giant teacup – before the image shatters into a pulsing series of random patterns.

Suddenly **MICHAEL** *appears on stage, struggling.* **DIRK** *and* **RICHARD** *launch themselves at him.*

MICHAEL What is happening? What are you doing?

DIRK It's working – we're contained in a nick in time! You have to hold it until his ship explodes.

REG *(making the abacus beads fly)* I'll try my best, but it's quite an incredible feat of mathematics. It will require all my concentration. Have you seen the custard creams?

On screen: The screen shows the ship beginning to take off, replaying the opening sequence.

MICHAEL I must save my people! I must avert the mistake. You cannot stop me – you are the mistake.

He begins to rant Coleridge frantically, providing a background wall of sound. He's desperate to break free, to get outside.

The upper air burst into life!
And a hundred fire-flags sheen,
To and fro they were hurried about!
And to and fro, and in and out,
The wan stars danced between.

And the coming wind did roar more loud,
And the sails did sigh like sedge;
And the rain poured down from one black cloud;
The Moon was at its edge.

The loud wind never reached the ship,
Yet now the ship moved on!
Beneath the lightning and the Moon
The dead men gave a groan.

Frantic piano music. Enter two workmen who run, Keystone Cops fashion, across stage carrying a sofa, and then exit...

DIRK Look Richard, there's your sofa – I knew it fitted in somewhere!

REG I can't hold it any longer... The beads canna take no more!

More smoke.

By now the noise is unbearable. A whooshing that has been building up for quite some time now spins out of control.

MICHAEL *breaks free and runs out into the maelstrom.*

There is an explosion and a scream.

Then silence and blackout.

EPILOGUE

SCENE TEN

DIRK's *office.* **DIRK** *is at his desk on the telephone.*

DIRK My dear Mrs. Sauskind. I can hardly tell you how much I have been looking forward to having this exact same conversation with you yet again. Where do you want to go today? Which particular item is it that you would like to discuss?

None of them? Your cat has never been missing? Dear Roderick passed away in your arms two years ago? You don't know who I am? Or why I should be sending you bills? But Mrs. Sauskind... ah, I understand – it's that bloody butterfly again... no, Mrs. Sauskind, I haven't lost a butterfly anymore than you have lost a cat. Its waveform has temporarily collapsed, that is all.

You see, Mrs. Sauskind, what you probably fail to appreciate is that it is as a direct result of my efforts that... If I might explain about the fundamental interconnectedness of all things... *(she hangs up.* **DIRK** *looks at the phone, slightly lost in thought)* Well, right you are, Mrs. Sauskind, you probably wouldn't have understood.

Janice!

PEARCE Yes, Mr. Gently?

He puts on his hat and begins to climb the stairs, returning to his opening position.

DIRK Kindly send out a revised bill, would you, to our dear Mrs. Sauskind. The new bill reads, "Saving human race from total extinction – no charge."

Curtain.

Act One - Scene One

Lighting

DIRK stands in darkness (p1)
He is lit as he strikes a match (p1)
A spotlight follows him (p2)
Lights up on DIRK's office (p2)
There is darkness (p3)

Sound/Effects

On screen: Animation Title Sequence – Like Star Wars, but done with blu-tac and felt tip pens.
"Douglas Adams's
DIRK GENTLY'S
HOLISTIC
DETECTIVE
AGENCY..." (p1)

Office sounds inter-mingling with more out-of-this world ones: howling wind, whirring photocopier, the screech of a hawk, the clattering of a typewriter, the neighing of a horse, the ringing of a telephone... (p2)

On screen: CAPTION: FOUR BILLION YEARS AGO... FRIDAY. A desolate, alien landscape gradually appears – the camera pans across rocks and boulders. The sky is bleak and forbidding. Nothing is living here. (p2)

On screen: The sky crackles with clouds, and there is rain. As the haze clears we begin to hear garbled radio instructions in an alien tongue. We see a spaceship, perched on a cliff edge. (p3)

The stage is flooded by smoke. A low, keening, electronic whine builds (p3)

On screen: The spaceship lifts itself off the ground, and hovers in a gathering electrical storm. There is a growing sound of tortured engines, building ominously. The ship hovers over the ground, distorts, and the whining noise oscillates. There is a blaring explosion which whites out the screen. (p3)

On stage: The chants cut off abruptly and there is darkness and silence. (p3)

Costume:

DIRK - He is dressed entirely in a long dark blue leather jacket, a red hat which fails to harmonise with it, and a suit which fails to harmonise with either: somehow he makes it cool (p1)

The stage is suddenly flooded by bizarrely dressed characters, clad in a strange cross between space suits and scuba diving kit. (p3)

Scene Two

Property List

Drinks (p4)

Dirk takes a drink from the tray (p4)

Drinks (p6)

Wine (p6)

Salt from a side table (p6)

Takes a pillow from a passing tray and mumbles into it (p6)

Offering a heavy silver salt cellar (p7)

Takes a dirty, small, Greek pot from her bag (p10)

Hat (p11)

Salt cellar (p11)

REG smashes pot, revealing the salt cellar embedded in it (p11)

Sound/Effects

A bell tolls (p4)

On screen caption: Senior Common Room, Thursday evening, Four billion years later. St. Cedd's College, Cambridge (p4)

On screen: Close-up surveillance photographs of Professor Urban Chronotis, from a variety of angles (p5)

On screen: Surveillance shots of RICHARD (p5)

On screen: College yearbook shots of DIRK. He appears ghoulish, drinking blood from a skull, in dark prayer over a black candle, and dangling upside-down. Beaming (p5)

REG performs an over-flamboyant and none-too-subtle piece of close-up magic: as RICHARD goes to take the salt cellar, it vanishes (p7)

Costume:

A number of formally clad guests at a pre-dinner drinks (p4)

RICHARD - He is wearing a coat, and dinner suit (p4)

PROFESSOR REG CHRONOTIS - similarly but far more shabbily dressed (as Richard) (p4)

SCENE THREE

Property List

In the corner is an old-fashioned landline and vintage answerphone (p13)

Cello (p13)

Mobile phone (p13)

Coffee table (p13)

Pot of tea (p13)

Cup of tea (p13)

Shoes (p15)

Perfume (p15)

Port decanter (p21)

Three glasses (p21)

SCENE FOUR

Property List

A coffee table on which is an old wooden abacus and, carefully set out, a decanter of port and three glasses. Piles of books everywhere (p16)

He pulls a chain of eleven paper clips and a small rubber swan out of RICHARD's nose (p17)

Book (p18)

Piece of paper (p18)

REG's entire body re-enters carrying tea tray in elaborate ceremony, tea cosy once again on head (p19)

He puts a sugar cube in his ear and twiddles with it (p19)

Carrot (p23)

Sound/Effects

On screen: An animated sofa appears. It is stuck in a stairwell, spinning in wireframe (p16)

Noises of kettle boiling (p17)

The kettle boils (p18)

On screen: close-up of book cover, reads – "Classical Greek Pots" (p18)

On screen: Close up of note, scribbly handwriting on crumpled paper "Regard this simple salt cellar, regard this simple hat" (p18)

There is a strange thumping noise from upstairs (p20)

Thumping heard again (p21)

A door is opened, and the thumping sound, which is becoming, but is not quite yet, identifiable, is heard again (p21)

Sound of door opening, then loud dramatic whinny and other unmistakable horse noises. There is a loud, pantomime toilet flush. (p23)

A neigh, not so violent this time, is heard (p23)

Costume:

Susan – is dressed formally for dinner (p13)

SCENE FIVE

Property List

Pair of binoculars (p24)

Mobile phone (p24)

Camera (p24)

Book (p27)

Lighting

A spotlight with a binocular-shaped filter scans the stage accordingly (p24)

Binoculars settle on the window of SUSAN's apartment as RICHARD climbs in through it (p24)

There is a flash (p24)

Spot on DIRK out (p25)

She switches the light on (p26)

Lights down (p29)

Sound/Effects

Landline rings (p24)

Key turns in the lock (p25)

Scene Six

Property List

Flashy convertible (p30)
Notes (p30)
Shotgun (p33)
Gordon's body (p33)
Petrol (p33)
Phone (p33)

Lighting

Lights up on Gordon's car (p30)
Sweeping headlights (p30)

Sound/Effects

The car hi-fi is playing Bach's English Suite No.2 in A minor. The music is in turn recorded by the answerphones of the various people GORDON calls in the course of this scene and is heard as a backdrop to his voice whenever the calls are replayed (p30)

Blaring horn (p30)

Susan's answerphone answers (p32)

A phone rings offstage (p33)

Fires both barrels into GORDON'S chest (p33)

A phone rings offstage (p33)

Costume:

Sergeant Gilks – plainclothes policeman

Gordon – gets up, dressed in a suit that would be immaculate if not for the large bloodstain on the shirt (p33)

Act Two – Scene One

Property List

With a vicious black felt-tip she is drawing mustachios and spectacles on a magazine poster (p34)

Newspaper (p34)

Large dictionary (p35)

Cigarette (p35)

She slams open the dictionary and starts to tear pages out of it, sending paper aeroplanes whizzing into the audience as DIRK deals with the call (p35)

Bag (p36)

French cigarettes (p36)

Pizza (p37)

Pulls down the blind (p40)

DIRK produces a metronome, with a silver tea-spoon strapped to the hand, and sets it ticking (p40)

Sound/Effects

Both desks have ringing phones on them. DIRK, exasperated, answers his and the ringing stops (p34)

Janice's extension rings (p34)

The phone rings again (p35)

On screen: A cat appears. A box appears around the cat. Also in the box is a lurid green vial of poison gas, and a lump of radioactive material (p38)

On screen: The box fills with gas, and the cat dies (p38)

On screen: The cat revives and looks annoyed (p38)

Scene Two

Property List

Body is zipped up into a body bag (p41)

Lighting

Lights gradually up on SUSAN's flat (p42)

Sound/Effects

On screen: A flashbulb pops, the picture of GORDON's dead face (p41)

Scene Three

Property List

Janice... emptying her desk (p44)
Dictionary (p45)
He opens the pizza box. A live rabbit is revealed. Dirk lifts it into a drawer (p45)
Dirk produces a Dictaphone and lets it play (p47)

Lighting

Lights gradually up (p44)
Lights up over this to show Dirk's office (p44)
Blackout, save for spot on Janice, on the telephone (p48)

Sound/Effects

Phone ringing (p44)

On screen: Surveillance pictures of the little girl with diagrammatic cutaways of her clothes flash up over this narration (p45)

RICHARD reacts strangely to DIRK's mention of his maiden aunt, starts suddenly, and then, moving slightly jerkily as if in a trance, he proceeds to perform an extravagant musical number, with as many other cast members as possible joining in. The specifics of the musical number do not matter. What does matter is that it is (a) completely unexpected (b) performed with genuine gusto and aplomb. At the end of the number, all except DIRK and RICHARD exit, RICHARD shakes himself out of his trance and sits looking a little dazed... (p47)

Janice's phone rings (p48)

Scene Four

Property List

Richard's flat - a main entrance and living area and an upstairs study filled with computers. A staircase, partially blocked by a sofa, connects the two (p49)

Hacksaw (p49)

Waste bin (p49)

He produces a magnifying glass and starts to burn ants with it, whilst fiddling with the computer and looking for the answerphone machine (p50)

Answerphone tape (p50)

Sound/Effects

Onscreen: the slowly rotating sofa (p49)

The tape plays. As it does, GORDON, dressed entirely in white, enters, near GILKS. He mouths along to the message. He is shot (on the tape), and jerks back. DIRK stops the tape (p52) GORDON'S RECORDED GHOST VOICE Susan, Susan, help me! Help me for God's sake. Susan, I'm dead... I'm dead... I'm dead and... I don't know what to do (p53)

Answerphone message – erased (p53)

Discordant howling sound-effect as GORDON runs around the room using new found poltergeist powers to fling books and furniture, mostly into the gallery at DIRK (p53)

Scene Five

Property List

Picks up a large sheet of paper, which is covered in blue felt-tip squiggle (p55)

Sound/Effects

Phone rings (p55)

Scene Six

Property List

Cello (p57)

Plate of pickled herrings and other half-eaten lunch things on the table (p57)

Ghost of his mobile phone (p57)

Sound/Effects

Landline rings (p57)

Security phone buzzes (p58)

Act Three – Scene One

Property List

Drinking from a saucer of milk and chewing on a realistic, dead mouse (p61)

Cigarette (p61)

Sound/Effects

On screen: The explosion and then the screen shows the DIRK logo, while some dramatic music plays, reminiscent of a Star Trek cliff-hanger (p62)

Gunshots (p62)

A car screeches. There is the sound of a car crash and more explosions (p62)

More explosions and a siren. A woman screams (p62)

More gunfire. A crescendo of an explosion (p62)

Scene Two

Property List

Coin (p63)

Tea (p65)

Sound/Effects

On screen:

Q: Is it possible to move back in time?

A: Yes.

Q: Is there any particular reason for one thing happening after another?

A: No.

Q: Is there anyway of stopping it?

A: Maybe (p67)

Dramatic chord (p67)

S<small>CENE</small> F<small>IVE</small>

Property List

Small children scatter rose petals etc. (p75)

Crossbow (p75)

Lighting

Blackout (p76)

Sound/Effects

Music plays (p75)

Church bells sound (p75)

The high-pitched whine of a crossbow bolt flying through the air is heard, then a thunk and a scream, and then the silence (p76)

Costume:

A wedding party, in full regalia, cross from stage left to stage right. The bride is radiant, the groom dashing...One guest (AL ROSS), in the rear of the procession, stops to tie his shoelace. (p75)

A mysterious tall stranger, dressed in oil-skins (p75)

Scene Six

Property List

Bag (p79)

Lighting

Blackout (p79)

Sound/Effects

There is a loud knock at the door (p79)
Dramatic chord (p79)

Scene Seven

Property List

Cello (p80)
Mobile phone (p80)

Sound/Effects

The music rises in volume and intensity (p80)
The answerphone beeps (p80)

Scene Eight

Property List

Coffee (p85)
Abacus (p86)
Sugar bowl (p86)
Plate (p87)

Sound/Effects

A howling wind arises (p86)

There are sounds – a roaring TARDIS, the Ride of the Valkyries, and a chiming clock. Stacks of books spin and whirl and the room dissolves in spinning furniture and smoke (p86)

On screen: Spinning clocks, whirling and merging, their hands wheeling out of control. Shots of clouds moving across the sky, merging into an endless tunnel of time. Briefly, a police box hurtles into view, and then is lost from sight (p86)

S<small>CENE</small> N<small>INE</small>

Property List

Tea (p88)
Crossbow (p89)
Mobile phone (p89)
Abacus (p92)

Lighting

Lights creep up (p88)
MICHAEL enters at the top of the stairs, in silhouette (p88)
Flashing lights (p92)
Blackout (p94)

Sound/Effects

Sound of a cup of tea being stirred (p88)

On screen: prehistoric landscape (p88)

Music: "Thus Spake Zarathustra" (p88)

The phone rings. (If possible, this is a duck phone, and so it quacks) (p98)

The tea things whirl around the room (p92)

There is smoke (p92)

On screen: The time tunnel appears again, but warped and twisted. Odd, alarmed objects shift through our field of vision – rubber ducks, double decker buses, a giant teacup – before the image shatters into a pulsing series of random patterns (p92)

On screen: The screen shows the ship beginning to take off, replaying the opening sequence (p92)

Frantic piano music (p92)

More smoke (p93)

By now the noise is unbearable. A whooshing that has been building up for quite some time now spins out of control (p93)

There is an explosion and a scream (p94)

Then silence (p94)

Costume:

MICHAEL - full scuba costume (p88)

Scene Ten

Property List

Hat (p95)

Sound/Effects

Curtain (p95)

Lightning Source UK Ltd.
Milton Keynes UK
UKHW00f1022190119
316379UK00006B/172/P